NOVICES:

A Study of Poetic Apprenticeship

By Clayton Eshleman:

Mexico & North (1962)
Residence on Earth (translations of Pablo Neruda) (1962)
The Chavin Illumination (1965)
State of the Union (translations of Aimé Césaire, with Denis Kelly) (1966)
Walks (1967)
Poemas Humanos/Human Poems (translations of César Vallejo) (1968)
Brother Stones (with William Paden's woodcuts) (1968)
Cantaloups & Splendor (1968)
T'ai (1969)
The House of Okumura (1969)
The House of Ibuki (1969)
Indiana (1969)
Yellow River Record (1969)
A Pitchblende (1969)
Bearings (1971)
Altars (1971)
A Caterpillar Anthology (editor) (1971)
Coils (1973)
Human Wedding (1973)
Spain, Take this Cup from Me (translations of Vallejo, with José Rubia Barcia)
    (1974)
Realignment (with drawings by Nora Jaffe) (1974)
The Gull Wall (1975)
Grotesca (1977)
On Mules Sent from Chavin (1977)
The Gospel of Celine Arnauld (1977)
The Name Encanyoned River (1978)
What She Means (1978)
César Vallejo: The Complete Posthumous Poetry (with José Rubia Barcia) (1978)
The Lich Gate (1980)
Nights We Put the Rock Together (1980)
Our Lady of the Three-Pronged Devil (1980)
Hades in Manganese (1981)
Antonin Artaud: Four Texts (with Norman Glass) (1982)
Visions of the Fathers of Lascaux (1983)
Fracture (1983)
Aimé Césaire: The Collected Poetry (with Annette Smith) (1983)
Given Giving (translations of Michel Deguy) (1984)
The Name Encanyoned River: Selected Poems 1960–1985 (1986)
Sea-Urchin Harakiri (translations of Bernard Bador) (1986)
Conductors of the Pit: Major Works by Rimbaud, Vallejo, Césaire, Artaud and Holan
    (1988)
Antiphonal Swing: Selected Prose 1962–1987 (1989)
Mistress Spirit (1989)
Hotel Cro-Magnon (1989)
Novices (1989)

NOVICES:
A Study of Poetic Apprenticeship

by Clayton Eshleman

Mercer & Aitchison   Los Angeles   1989

Acknowledgements

Chapters of this study have appeared in the following publi-
cations: *Agni, Antiphonal Swing: Selected Prose 1962–1987* by
Clayton Eshleman (McPherson & Co., Kingston NY, 1989),
and *Sulfur*.

Again, my gratitude to my closest reader, Caryl Eshleman, for
constructive criticism and suggestions during the writing of
this study.

ISBN 0-923980-20-2 (signed ltd.)
ISBN 0-923980-21-0 (hardcover trade)
ISBN 0-923980-22-9 (softcover trade)

for George Butterick

Thou hast a lap full of seed,
And this is a fine country.
Why dost thou not cast thy seed
And live in it merrily?
                    —William Blake, 1793

I came to see that art, as it was understood
until 1800, was henceforth finished, on its last
legs, doomed, and that so-called artistic activity
with all its abundance is only the many-formed
manifestation of its agony.
                    —attributed (falsely it turned
                    out) to Picasso, and probably
                    written by Giovanni Papini, in
                    the early 1950s

These two "statements" drove lightning and rain through me as an apprentice to poetry, in Kyoto, in the early 1960s. It was as if I worked daily under the spell of personal potency and transpersonal impotency. Today still looking at the statements I see a propeller twist and then whirr, and in the haze of bladed motion the melding of yes and no that probably every young artist in most ages and places has had to stare at for many years, as he flexes in place, extending and contracting his claws . . .

For years I have wanted to make a trenchant declaration to those who are on the verge of an apprenticeship to poetry. I am not interested in being prescriptive, or rehearsing poetic terminology. I want to do here what the Introduction to Poetry textbooks *don't* do: to address the initial chaos as well as the potential coherence involved in making a commitment to poetry, and suggest that blocks and chasms are not to be avoided but are to be worked through and assimilated.

On one level, we are all belated comers to that labyrinth in whose folds struggle between self and other is said to lead to the tranformation of personality and significant art. On another level, the world now seems deeper and wider and more vector-permeated than ever before. Through the efforts of much multiply-based writers as Ezra Pound, Antonin Artaud, and Charles Olson, the image of the poet has been densified and removed from the academic-literary niche which had come to mean that the poet was merely a clever manipulator of his own sensitivity rather than a man or woman of knowledge.

What I intend to stress here is the most soulful and open image of the poet that I can grasp—an image that is involved with years of apprenticeship within the confines of a social structure that offers superficial hand-outs and massive undermining. These pages are for the young person who desires that impossible state identified by Artaud in the asylum at Rodez: "The great total dimension is to become as a simple man strong as all infinity."

Chapter 1

(Charles Olson to Cid Corman, January 26, 1953)

"you must cease to think of a poem as anything but an expression of
THAT WHICH YOU ARE A SPECIALIST—which has to be, if it is a
poem, YRSELF, YR THINGS, no one else's, nothing else but that
which you are SURE of

              and you must be prepared to find that you have
LITTLE to speak of: that, surprisingly enuf, is what we all find—that—
as The Confuser sd—it's all/as much/as on the back of a postage
stamp

      CLEARLY, you are writing abt what you think are the proper sub-
jects of writing—not at all abt one, CID CORMAN:

                  please *hear* me. I
am giving you a present. It's yrself.

                We Americans have nothing but our
personal details. Don't let anyone fool you, any poet, any body. There
is nothing but all the details, sensations, facts which are solely known
to Cid Corman. And you must stick to them—get them straight—even
if (AS IT DAMN WELL IS) NOTHING. Understand? It will seem—
does seem to you—NOTHING: that is

              why you are writing abt anything
but CORMAN. Because Corman to Corman is ZERO

                 what you don't
know is, that that is as it is for anyone but the pseudo-whatever:

                 that we
begin with ZERO—are O."[1]

Olson's ZERO is also the filled pot of yourself. You are stuffed
as well as empty. Perhaps you approach poetry, desirous of
being effected by it, because the friction between your impac-
tion and your emptiness has become unbearable—because you
seek to bear it, bear the friction and as in the image of giving
birth, be reborn, bear yourself—

Artaud:

And there is only one sun, one moon and stars because everyone yielded on this point about universal light to the concep-

tions of that phenomenal hood named god, instead of doing as in the real world where each individual enlightens himself on himself, as did Van Gogh in order to paint the night with his 12 candled hat.

None will initiate me into anything.

All experience is resolutely personal.[2]

A few years earlier, Artaud had also written:

We have never written anything except against a backdrop of the incarnation of the soul, but the soul already is made (and not by ourselves) when we enter into poetry.[3]

The charge is to enlighten yourself on yourself, to refuse continuing initiation by parents and teachers, but the contradiction (to be ingested, not stopped before) is that the discovery of poetry is also the discovery that the soul of the world has already been formed—it is an immense and detailed rose window made up of all the initiations and stories of imaginative art. It in fact includes stories and figures you will never know about because they are in languages (or places) that you will never read (or see). The cathedral was built way before you arrived. But you are not here to worship—

Robert Kelly:

The typical mistake of religion has been to assume that what the priest does at the altar is somehow transmittable to me, poor dumb me sitting in the pew, kneeling there with my mouth open, that somehow some magic that he can perform in Latin or with his hands or in Mithra with a cut bull can transform me. And the superstition that lies there forgets that I must do something too; even if the magic part works I am transformed, but 10 minutes later my transformation falls off me just as I dry out after coming in from the rain. I mean, it may be real rain in that church, maybe that's real blood, but somehow my habits are sufficient to drain that out again, purify my animal nature. I think the poem gets harder in the way that a religion, if it were a real thing, would be a hard thing because it would inevitably be personal, it would inevitably be something *you* have to do & *I* have to do. That if I'm given a poem which tells me the whole thing I have no work to do with it. It can't save me then. I don't know exactly what I have to be saved from, but let's allow salvation for a moment—I can't be saved unless I do it myself. And I think poems become hard exactly as religion fades away—because we've got to get the sense that nothing is really easy. There's a certain kind of person who will inevitably go to *The Cantos* or the *Maximus Poems* or some other ballbuster and make that his destiny for a year or two years, who recognizes however dumb he is when he starts out, there is something in this complexity that if he just go through it, if he follows the dance or the pattern or climbs the rock, he will have passed through a process which is not just a process of perception or critical judgement but a process of transformation.[4]

Notes

1. Charles Olson, Letters for Origin (1950–1956), NYC, 1970, pp. 119–120. This edition, which contains only portions of Olson's letters to Cid Corman, and none of Corman's to Olson, is now out of print, and has been superseded by *Charles Olson & Cid Corman: The Complete Correspondence, 1950–1964*, Volume 1 (Orono, Maine, 1987), edited and annotated by George Evans (Volume 2 is due out spring 1989). In Olson's body of work (as in Rilke's and van Gogh's, for example) correspondence is a major element; in fact, at many points there is no genre difference between his poetry, letters, and essays. Concerning other important Olson correspondences, see footnote 1, chapter 13, and *Charles Olson & Robert Creeley: The Complete Correspondence*, edited and annotated by George Butterick, eight volumes of which have been published by Black Sparrow Press.

2. Antonin Artaud, *Letter to André Breton*, Sparrow 23, Santa Barbara, 1974. See the Note prefacing this letter for the particular initiation that occasioned Artaud's protest against all initiations.

3. *Antonin Artaud Anthology*, San Francisco, 1965, p. 100.

4. "Ta'wil or How to Read," Vort #5, 1974, p. 140.

Chapter 2

In alchemical terminology, which also applies to writing poetry, prime or first matter is to be found in yourself. It is the
uncreated, the *masa confusa*.[1] To be confused is to be inert;
inertia is the primary sin, the dragon to be slain. You cut apart
to name, to say that it is this and not that. In the *masa confusa*
(your self, your ZERO = your uroboros, the swamp of your attempts at thought and emotional clarity) are all the seeds of
what is to come.

The desire to write poetry leads first to seeing the *vilifigura*,
the reviled face, the shame of your own face.[2] To embrace your
soul may be to experience the extent to which you despise your
soul, the extent to which whatever this soul is feels despised—
for what have you actively asked of it before? Isn't it true that
it has been left in the corner for years, collecting dust like a
castaway doll? Loathing itself, its first motion upon suddenly
being awakened may be to claw out at the one who has dis-
turbed its remorseful holding-pattern (and the clawed one may
very well claw out at others; to suddenly wake up may mean
fury at having been asleep so long e.g., Malcolm X in prison).

When I considered attempting to evade this turbulent, sick-
ening confusion in Kyoto, 1963,[3] I saw I was faced with an
alternative worse than confronting it, for that alternative
seemed to consist in my attaching myself to another poet's
leavings and saying: this will be my poem. Had I settled for
this, I would have been proclaiming that my soul was so sick
that I had to mask it with the soul of another, a soul-mask tried
and successful (published, heralded, anthologized, conse-
crated by critics and scholars). With a lot of hard, unsatisfying,
imitative work, this might have led to becoming a spoken
cipher (instead of a ZERO), a diminuition of another's
energies.

It is natural to feel competitive with one's peers. But one is
essentially not in competition with other poets. One is essentially only in competition with one's own death.

Alchemy suggests that to not evade the *masa confusa* is to search for that which can withstand dissolution and fire, that which experiences events as psychic process. Just to discover one's own resistances is something—to feel something push back when one pushes out (Olson later in the quoted-from letter to Corman writes: "that's what a poem is, a conjecture abt an experience we are, for what reason, seized by—BUT I MEAN SEIZED. It has to be something on our mind, really on our mind, at the heart of us—where it hurts").

> *Moonset, Gloucester,*
> *December 1, 1957, 1:58 AM*
>
> Goodbye red moon
> In that color you set
> west of the Cut I should imagine
> forever Mother
>
> After 47 years this month
> a Monday at 9 AM
> you set I rise I hope
> a free thing as probably
> what you more were Not
> the suffering one you sold
> sowed me on Rise
> Mother from off me
> God damn you God damn me my
> misunderstanding of you
>
> I can die now I just begun to live[4]

It is the unpoetic, the anti-poetic, that encloses the precious material—your actual thoughts while writing, what you want to overlook, the awkward, the ugly, thoughts that make you feel ashamed. What *do* you resist while writing? Does your mother swim forth and call you to bed? Do you recall with pleasure a perverse humiliation that took place when you were three? Do "bad words" mosquito your working space? Do you *want* to write and *need* to shit?

César Vallejo:

> *Intensity and Height*
>
> I want to write, but out comes spume,
> I want to say so much and I lurch in mud;

there's no spoken cipher which is not a sum,
there's no written pyramid, without interior bud.

I want to write, but I feel puma;
I want to laurel myself, but I utter onions.
There's no sproken cough which doesn't end in brume,
there is no god nor son of god, without evolution.

Because of this let's go, then, and feed on herbs,
lamentation flesh, ululation fruit,
our melancholy soul in preserve.

Let's go! Let's go! I'm wounded;
let's go and consume that already consumed
let's go, blackbird, and fecundate your ladybird.[5]

Vallejo's resolution of this sonnet is less based on the idea of
abandoning the frustrations of writing for sexual release (or
death, if one reads "crow" as a death emblem), than it is on
calling upon the animal powers of his imagination to redirect
the physical blockage. The underpinning of this piece, as well
as much of Vallejo's mature poetry, is the poet's acute sensitivity to the suffering of others, and his refusal to forget about it
while writing.

Reflecting on the figure of Enion, in Blake's *The Four Zoas*,
Northrop Frye writes:

> She is the "vain shadow of hope" which finds everything short
> of a complete apocalypse hopeless. She is the part of our minds
> which dimly realizes that all pleasure is at least partly a dream
> under an anesthetic. Something is always suffering horribly
> somewhere, and we can only find pleasure by ignoring that
> fact. We must ignore it up to a point, or go mad; but in the
> abyss of consciousness, to which Enion has been banished,
> there lurks the feeling that joy is based on exclusion, that the
> Yule log can blaze cheerfully only when the freezing beggars in
> the streets are, for the moment, left to freeze.[6]

The peristalic body of a poetry, visionary *and* critical (of its
own insights as well as of the world) cannot be regularly
rhythmic, cannot simply "flow," as long as the innocent suffer.
I break my teeth on Apollo as long as my taxes issue forth as a
blowtorch into the face of a Latin-American peasant. I swallow and I break. Broken and loaded. Symmetry implies per-
fection and is a lie as long as the world body is broken, tor-
tured, in separation, and utterly (now) imperiled: "Fighting

World War II took the equivalent of three megatons of TNT: all that and more now fits into the business end of a single MX missile."[7]

Notes

1. Material on alchemy is taken from notes made listening to a James Hillman seminar on alchemy, Los Angeles, 1985; during Hillman's two days of lectures, I jotted down the basic outline for *Novices*. The key work on psychology and alchemy is C. G. Jung's *Mysterium Coniunctionis*. For material on the uroboros, see the first chapter of Erich Neumann's *The Origins and History of Consciousness*. For a critique of Neumann and an enlarged sense of the uroboros, see Wolfgang Giegerich's "Deliverance from the Stream of Events: Okeanos and the Circulation of the Blood," *Sulfur* #21, 1988.

2. Diane Wakoski evokes the insidious strength of the *vilifigura* in "I have had to learn to live with my face" (from *The Motorcycle Betrayal Poems*, NYC, 1971):

> I want to go to sleep and never wake up.
> The only warmth I ever feel is wool covers on a bed.
> But self-pity could trail us all, drag us around on the bottom
> of shoes like squashed snails so that
> we might never fight / and it is anger I want now, fury,
> to direct at my face and its author,
> to tell it how much I hate what it's done to me,
> to contemptuously, sternly, brutally even, make it live with
>   itself,
> look at itself every day,
> and remind itself
> that reality is
> learning to live with what you're born with,
> noble to have been anything but defeated . . .

Another more transpersonal engagement with the sourness of self and background, as they thrust themselves upon the novice, is illustrated in Section V of Robert Kelly's "The Exchanges" (*origin #5*, second series), as an omnipresent "black flower" that accompanies the poet everywhere.

3. See my *Coils* (Los Angeles, 1973). In his 1972 Preface to *Caesar's Gate*, Robert Duncan writes:

> I had, and still have—for again and again the apprehension re-
> turns—essential to my art, a horror of creation, as if beauty were
> itself the sign of an immanent danger. The announcement then
> of an imminent disclosure. It is the grue, the sense of coming near
> to grief, that signifies in the lore of Scotch folk, the wierd of po-
> etry. My art sought to spell that moment, even as I saw Peggy

Linnet [an artist whose drawings were the symptom or flowering of a schizophrenic breakdown] in her art sought to dispell. In her house the vividness of that borderline of spelling and dispelling was felt as a kind of sea-sickness, a vertigo at the heart of the continent, the discovery of a discontinuity in the mass we would take experience to be, a poetic nausea.

I had come to the pass in 1949 when I committed myself to Poetry, even as if to a madhouse or a religion. Yet it was a madness I had to make up, a conviction that I came to know only as I went into the depths of its invention in which I stood convicted of being its author. In the fiction of that authority I was without the guarantees of the authenticity I saw in madness. What Peggy Linnet suffered I projected. The grue was there, yes. A suspicion in poetry was growing in me. I would have, ultimately, to name the grief myself.

In another context, commenting on Artaud's ability to articulate excitations intolerable to his imagination, Duncan wrote: "We can be entertained by what he suffered." (*Letters*, Highlands, North Carolina, 1958)

4. Charles Olson, *The Distances*, NYC, 1960.

5. *Conductors of the Pit: Major Works by Rimbaud, Vallejo, Césaire, Artaud, and Holan* (translated by Clayton Eshleman), NYC, 1988, p. 43.

6. Northrop Frye, *Fearful Symmetry*, Princeton, 1969, p. 279.

7. *Newsweek*, March 2, 1987, p. 72.

Chapter 3

In a "visionary moment dramatic" of the 7th Night of *The Four Zoas*, Blake writes:

> Los embrac'd the Spectre, first as a brother,
> Then as another Self, astonish'd, humanizing & in tears,
> In Self abasement Giving up his Domineering lust.

You are not who you think you are, you are something to be imagined. Your inertia, your *masa confusa*, is your spectre, and your spectre is not only to be scrutinized and cut apart, it is to be accepted and embraced. I am not my background, the novice cries, I am not merely a mass of assignments, restrictions, impulses, and black thoughts about others—but once I subtract all these—what do I have? At this point, poetry intensifies its glow on the horizon. I am that, the novice cries out again, I am those words of e. e. cummings, Dylan Thomas, Pablo Neruda, Rimbaud.

But in practice, to believe that one is the words others have found in the struggle to say themselves, is to screw one's ZERO onto the nozzle of a hose through which only others are pouring. At this point, there is the possibility of turning back to what of oneself has been rejected and saying: but I am that, on one important level, I am what I have been given and shaped into. This is the only wood I really have to put into the fireplace.

Then the novice possibly turns again to the smoldering horizon and understands something about the enormity of his task. His possible small fire is a joke compared to the dragon of flames emanating from the multi-chambered sun of achieved imagination—but at least he is holding his own log, and seeing that in essence his tiny fire may be of the same nature as the great one out there.

It all smarts so much, this burning water, this "thing" made up of irresolvable contradictions, this "thing" that is so much

bigger than any combed-out "truth." The liquid spilling
through the hose is flame; the most distant fire can be tapped
right here. As he squats by the blazing red drops, this novice
glimpses that making use of another's poetry is a double if not
a triple bladed gesture. Since he only has his background to
draw upon, he tries to think through its interstices, and hears
himself murmuring, as if between waking and sleep:

> Come forth that I may slay you, father, and, slung across my
> shoulder, may your blood drip into my lute. I will call my slay-
> ing an embrace, and as I slay-embrace you, I will pocket a few
> of your organs, and reject the rest. I will call your marbles gems,
> and your gems marbles. And I will try to shuffle you into the
> deck of what I call my experience in the context of my times.

As he attempts to read "between the lines," to induct a
poem's full connotational field, he notices that the lines do not
want to yield, there seems to be no place for him between lines
1 and 2, or between 2 and 3, or 3 and 4. Perhaps he recalls, in
his frustration, having read a version of the beginning of everything, with God separating the heavens from the waters of the
deep. That God now seems to be a little like him, a son of God,
a second-comer, trying to separate the lines from their own intense embrace—to push up a heaven line and pull an earth
line down a bit, to make a place for little Me. Each act of reading as a writer becomes for this novice an attempt at incision
into a primal scene.

He begins to realize, this novice I am dreaming of, that he
must look long and hard at coitus in order to escape intellectual inhibition, for coitus is everywhere he looks—in bridge
and windmill, furnace and vault—it is the recombining
magma into which as a dreamer he is dipped, as if by animal
tongs. In comparison to most poets, the Freudian ethnogra-
phers look bold—but then again, this novice thinks, they are
not watching their own hands dissolve in burning liquid as I
am—they have a distance—I am up against my own body as
my hedge and hinge. And he continues to think: why do most
poets appear to fear the lower body? Why does he have to go
to N. O. Brown's *Love's Body* to find a clot like

> One of Melanie Klein's discoveries in the world of the uncon-
> scious is the archetypal—primordial and universal—fantasy of

(parental) coitus as a process of mutual devouring—oral cop-
ulation; or rather, cannibalistic; and therefore combining in
one act the two Oedipal wishes, parental murder and incest;
and including sexual inversion, since the male member is always seen as a breast sucked.[1]

To dwell on the grotesque with its chambers of warped, self-
distorting mirrors, may be to increase the possibility of passing
through a bottleneck that ultimately leads back to the world
outside the novice, but a world which now has the novice inside it, as if he is in what he is looking at. For the primal scene
parents are the "secretaries" of two sets of parents, the four
grandparents, etc. From this viewpoint, the primal scene is
buried at the base of the pyramid upon whose peak the novice
thinks of himself as an individual. Turn the pyramid on its side,
novice, and enter its peak. Who knows what you will find at
the back wall—deified ancesters, human beings with animal
heads, or roaring nothingness? And streaming out from the
base, like giant squid tentacles, are these not the pyramid's
roots connecting it to the kingdoms of the nonhuman other?

Gaston Bachelard, pondering Lautréamont, writes: there is
"a *need* to *animalize* that is at the origins of imagination. The
first function of imagination is to create animal forms."[2]

N. O. Brown, digesting Sandor Ferenczi's *Thalassa* as an as-
pect of *Love's Body*:

> Copulation is uterine regression. "The purpose of the sex act
> can be none other than an attempt to return to the mother's
> womb." "The sex act achieves this transitory regression in a
> three-fold manner: the whole organism attains this goal by
> purely hallucinatory means, somewhat in sleep; the penis, with
> which the organism as a whole has identified itself, attains it
> partially or symbolically; while only sexual secretion itself pos-
> sesses the prerogative, as representative of the ego and its nar-
> cissistic double, the genital, of attaining *in reality* to the womb
> of the mother."

> Life itself is a catastrophe, or fall, or trauma. The form of the
> reproductive process repeats the trauma out of which life arose,
> and at the same time endeavors to undo it. The "uterine re-
> gressive trend in the sex act" is an aspect of the universal goal
> of all organic life—to return to the lifeless condition out of
> which life arose.[3]

Notes

1. N. O. Brown, *Love's Body*, NYC, 1966, p. 25.

2. Gaston Bachelard, *Lautréamont*, Dallas, 1986, p. 27.

3. *Love's Body*, pp. 47 and 53. I refer to the novice as "he" because I am writing out of my male experience. I mention this at this point for several reasons. Most of the sources here come from male writers because, as a novice myself in 1960, the artistic international field seemed overwhelmingly rich and it did not occur to me at that time to question the fact that this richness was also overwhelmingly male. I became aware while studying the *I Ching* in Kyoto in 1962 that the yin/yang differentiation associated man with day/clarity/good and woman with night/opaqueness/bad. This made me doubt its wisdom and it also helped me to start opening myself to "the darkening of the light," i.e., to powers that my critique of the *I Ching* made me realize I had previously been unaware of. I was so pent upon myself at the time that it did not occur to me to start investigating the implications of all this in terms of culture and society. Since the early 1970s, my poetry has hammered at patriarchal sexuality, constantly attempting to block reader-escape from the fact that men usurp "self," mis-use their strength against women (and against themselves), equate terror with glory and heroism, and control nearly all the power junctures in society. In this regard, I am in near agreement with Andrea Dworkin in her compelling book, *Pornography*. The reader might therefore inquire: why do you quote Ferenczi, then, where he not only restricts coitus to a male viewpoint, but treats woman as no more than a conduit by which man attempts "to return to the mother's womb?" [And while their feel for the human is quite different, Ferenczi's view is not incompatible with that of Aleister Crowley for whom woman's body is no more than a "pylon" through which man might make contact with the infinite. In this regard, Tantrik sexuality might seem to exploit while Christian sexuality represses.] My response to the question above is the following: Ferenczi is still valuable because whether he intends to or not he unmasks male fantasy, and contributes his own speck of information about the nature of that living midden called the self. To what extent primordial impulses to penetrate/attack/fantasize belong to the male sphere I cannot and would not say. And while all of us should encourage women to explore realms that have previously (i.e., in historical time) been dominated by masculine compulsions and maps, men should not simply evade these truly loaded words, such as "masculinity" and "phallus" etc. All of us, I feel, are still in the rudimentary stages of exploring (and when necessary, dismantling) that gargantuan "I" that is not only a landmine but also the repository for much of our feeling of love and public trust. Too much avant-garde or experimental art appears to regard this grotesque "combined object" in a way that is evoked (in a different context, of course) by John Ashbery in his poem "Soonest Mended":

And Angelica, in the Ingres painting, was considering
the colorful but small monster near her toe, as though wondering whether forgetting
The whole thing might not, in the end, be the only solution.

Chapter 4

Everything is material. You must learn to turn any flinch or fantasy into grist so as not to be bound to your own backside. You make a gain on your material when you are able to express that which you do not know, which, at the same time, seems welded to that which you feel you are. To pull up a fistful of crabgrass and feel the whole yard tremble. To lift a rock and see deep into the iguana's eyes.

The imagination as I understand it is synthesis in melee, melee in synthesis. Images are winding windows.

Arthur Rimbaud argued in 1871 that the poet via an ordered derangement of the senses must make himself monstrous[1] (here I read not only "freakish," but "marvelous," "prodigious," based on the Latin *monstrare*, to show—suggesting that the poem is a full or amplified showing, to the extent that it becomes grotesque, beyond observational limits). I would footnote Rimbaud's statement with: and the imagination must become mongrel, freed of racial stratification, released from the prism of white supremacy,[2] whose self-reflecting facets include purity, sanctity, spirituality, sublimity, forever, and God.

You sit down with the intention of saying something nice about someone you love. Before your fingers can touch the keys, an inversion takes place: a worm peers out of the apple, or something merely irrelevant falls like a veil across your intended address. Psyche has cautiously opened her bedroom door and glanced into the hallway; she has responded to your intention by turning it upside down, or by making it sound irrelevant, or dumb. She will stay in the doorway for a moment, seeing if you bite. If you can absorb and immediately assimilate her inversion, she may smile, and her smile may crack your line in two. Chances are you will disregard her query, and she will shut the door, at which point you will mush on through your intended program, the prisoner of your intention, going through its paces, resolute, predictable, over before it has begun. You will have a limited number of chances with Psyche and her door. Too many initial closures and she will abandon you to *closure as a routine*, which might be defined in the following way: poetry as reification/reinforcement of what has taken place in the past. The past as citadel, imagination its court life—the present as heretical, that which is to be swept out of sight, the refuse. The door Psyche opens is a breach between walled-off present and walled-off past. Her desire is to have intercourse with the poet, to slip out the Puritan plank between her resting place and his.

Linear time, Puritanic time. The "light at the end" to justify this struggle, this now. But such "light" is a haze, is nothing, is distraction from the here and now. When I focus on my literal death my glance drifts to a vanishing point. Tunnel vision is no vision. Instead, populate the tunnel with bathing shelves, bring in the rats. Let's gnaw into a bask, corrode the relaxed sides of the image, set in stained glass, alcoves with access to the Hitlers of the heart, our dread of vanishing, our need to plug up our hole and by doing so, banish all difference, all otherness . . . all that does not reinforce our uniqueness. Alas, but hooray, we are not unique. Unlike trees, we are adrift in a breath bowl, rootless algae, wings searching for angelic bodies.

Notes

1. Best summation of Rimbaud's achievement I know of is Kenneth Rexroth's 5 pages on him in *Classics Revisited*.
2. See James Hillman's "Notes on White Supremacy," *Spring* 1986.

Chapter 5

My first poem was called "The Outsider," and was a timid, versified re-enactment of the feelings I had picked up reading Colin Wilson's *The Outsider*, a book which introduced me to the visionary figure on the periphery of societal centers, in 1957. However, my first engagement with poesis took place when I was a freshman at Indiana University, 1953, in Herbert Stern's Freshman Composition class. After having given us several assignments (which I had done poorly with), he said: write anything you want to.

I wrote a kind of prose-poem, in the voice of an aging prostitute, standing at her hotel window, watching newspaper and rubbish blow down a deserted street at 4 AM. Stern gave me an A– and under the grade wrote: *see me*. When I sat down in his office, he told me that the piece was excellent but that I was in trouble because I had not written it. I still recall his words: "the person who wrote this did not write your other themes." I protested and in the end he believed me, and said: "if you can write like that, there are a couple of books you should read." On a scrap of paper, which he handed me, he wrote: *The Metamorphosis*, and under it, *Portrait of the Artist as a Young Man*. To what extent Stern himself was conscious of the significance of this particular juxtaposition, I will never know—but by citing the Kafka story (which I waited two years to read), he had identified what had happened to me in my "free theme," and by citing Joyce (which I read nine years later), had he offered me the challenge to become an artist?

In my theme I had aged myself, changed my sex, and dressed up as a parody of my mother. The figure was utterly fictional— I knew nothing about prostitutes, and that was probably part of the point too: contra Olson, I had entered imagination by speaking out of a place I had never personally experienced. I had left the confines of an "assignment"—my entire life up to that time and then some was framed by assignments—and wandered into an "other." *Je est un autre*, Rimbaud had written when he was 17. I am a metaphor. Clayton is a prostitute, Clayton is not merely Clayton. Clayton does not merely live in the Phi Delta Theta fraternity house and take abuse daily as a "pledge." Clayton is a 55 year old woman looking out on a street that does not exist.

A move toward origin. Toward our so-called "face before birth." Toward that which we are but will never be. Toward what we were but are not. The initial fascination with writing poetry is similar to a visit to an astrologer and a request for a horoscope. My aged whore positioned me toward a past in the present, indicating (though I did not realize it then) continuity and depth. The street was empty except for blowing (unreadable) newspapers, yesterday's news. It was empty and I was to populate it with my own news—I was to learn how to read the street, and to get used to not being myself. I was, like a tree still rooted in Indiana earth, to learn how to twist within my own bark and observe "other" things around me.

Chapter 6

When I was teaching at the California Institute of the Arts
in 1971, I had writing students who were smoking a lot of dope
and taking LSD. I wanted to move them further in and further
out,[1] to help them become more inward and more outward,
because conventional recognitions (the enemy of imaginative
perceptions) live on a threshold between careful observation
and proprioceptive awareness, drugs or no drugs. Ultimately,
as the phrase "imaginative awareness" is intended to suggest,
poetic mind moves so rapidly between the inner and the outer
that in many cases (Montale and Vallejo come immediately to
mind) the distinction appears to be eliminated.

The outer-oriented exercise at Cal Arts made use of objects
in conjunction with texts by Francis Ponge.[2] I brought fruit,
paintings, and things like an art-nouveau ash-tray, into the
class-room, put them one at a time on the table, and asked the
students to simply look at the object for 15 minutes and then
to write a paragraph of what they had seen. We read and discussed Ponge's prose-poems on a boat, an oyster, wine, or rain,
etc., as examples of permeative observation. Initially, many
student paragraphs were so disoriented that the object itself
was not present. Some students who applied themselves and
took the course a second semester improved considerably. One
day I brought a bottle of 1962 Brane-Cantenac to class; we all
went outside and sitting in a circle, sipping the wine, commented on what it said to us when we lolled it in our mouths;
then I asked the students to write down what they associated
with the taste of the wine.

The inner-oriented exercise was more complicated, and almost impossible to do in class. I had been struck by a phrase
that the painter Francis Bacon used in a BBC conversation
with David Sylvester. When asked how he arrived at his images, Bacon responded that they often came from "semi-
conscious, or subliminal scanning." I understood this to mean
that Bacon worked in a kind of trance between waking and

dreaming, where things decompose, merging and fraying with memories and sensations. I have trained myself to write in such a state, encouraging image-chains to proliferate, so as to not will the poem but in a way that is hard to explain, to accompany it on its way. There is an alchemical image of a man semi-reclined, watching with intense interest a tree which has grown out of his groin. That image is a stunning example of the self-connectedness *and* otherness of art as I understand it.

One problem at Cal Arts was: how get the students to notice and to articulate psychic processes?[3] I asked them to try free-associating out loud in class, and to follow the associations as well as the sounds of the words. Everyone began by stammering out disconnected gerunds and/or nouns, like "sun . . . clouds . . . flying . . . dreaming . . . moon . . . bird . . ." which indicated to me that censorship was extremely active in the intervals between the words, and that the uttered words were ones which had passed the acceptable-as-images-of-myself test. It was impossible for anyone to keep the exercise going, even in a halting state, for more than a minute. When I asked people to put in "I/s," to encourage a more self-involved participation, most students would stop after a few seconds and say they couldn't continue. The few that kept at it uttered clichés and pieces of advertising jargon and expressed amazement that when they tried to free-associate out loud clichés and jargon were what came out. They seemed to have no ability to put together word combinations that were in any sense spontaneously unusual. We discussed Allen Ginsberg's little aphorism, "First thought, best thought," and spent a lot of time pondering what was and what was not a thought.

To a certain extent, it was the *vilifigura* thumbing its nose in the silences between stammered out words, a fear of revealing material to peers and to me. I think this touches on the core problem of the creative writing workshop: peer pressure encourages the throwing up of defenses—justifications, rationalizations, hurt feelings—rather than the lowering of them so as to enable Psyche to make some unexpected gestures in the poems-to-be. I asked the students to try the exercise alone at home on a cassette recorder and try to detect "holes" in patterns, ways in to their concerns, as if they were a halfback, the football suddenly snapped into their hands; the play has misfired and they must immediately find an alternative hole in the wall of advancing defense.

From 1969 to 1973, I practiced this exercise myself, alone with a cassette. While I never used taped sequences per se in poems, I think the practice loosened me up and made me more daring in admitting fascinating *and* irrelevant (at the moment of presentation) words while writing. Such chains as "ale the heil in to roo the bovine sky over what roots," or "hear the ore masted in the world Ulyssean siren wax," made me more flex- ible and porous to sounds and associations (bovine sky, ore masted) which enable poems to veer and recharge, making lit- tle leaps between "the clashing rocks" of the conventional and the insignificant (that defensive wall in which holes must be found in order to really run and, as Robert Duncan once put it, exercise one's faculties at large).

Notes

1. The idea that conventional poetry fails to thrust in or thrust out was brought to my attention by Olson's "*Outside, Inside*: Notes on Narra- tive, provoked by Mr. Creeley's stories," which appeared in *New Di- rections* annual #13, 1951.

2. At Cal Arts I used Cid Corman's Ponge versions (*Things*, NYC, 1971); since then, Beth Archer's translation of some of the same poems as well as others has appeared (*The Voice of Things*, NYC, 1974). Both translations are acceptable, and rather than choosing between them, it is more useful to read a Corman version and an Archer version of the same poem together with a French-English dictionary, looking up words the translators disagree upon. In this connection, see the issues of *Caterpillar* magazine (1967–1973), where 10 "Tests of Translation" (modeled upon Louis Zukofsky's A *Test of Poetry*) appeared.

3. Besides the two exercises discussed here, there was a third, in the form of a reading/writing notebook that I have continued to make use of for over 15 years. Students are asked to draw a horizontal line across each page of a large notebook, and to keep the notebook open by any book of poetry they are reading. Quotations go in the top half; response in the bottom half. The idea here is to break down the distance between reading and writing, and to encourage the student to start poems while reading as well as to turn from a stalled piece of his own writing back to a text he had previously been reading.

Chapter 7

The alchemist Fulcanelli:

> The picture of the labyrinth is thus offered to us as emblematic of the whole labour of the Work, with its two major difficulties, one the path which must be taken in order to reach the centre—where the bitter combat of the two natures takes place—the other the way which the artist must follow in order to emerge. It is there that *the thread of Ariadne* becomes necessary for him, if he is not to wander among the winding paths of the task, unable to extricate himself.[1]

Anton Ehrenzweig:

> Any creative search, whether for a new image or idea, involves the scrutiny of an often astronomical number of possibilities. The correct choice between them cannot be made by a conscious weighing up of each single possibility cropping up during the search; if attempted it would only lead us astray. A creative search resembles a maze with many nodal points. From each of these points many possible pathways radiate in all directions leading to further crossroads where a new network of high- and by-ways comes into view. Each choice is equally crucial for further progress. The choice would be easy if we could command an aerial view of the entire network of nodal points and radiating pathways still lying ahead. This is never the case. If we would map out the entire way ahead, no further search would be needed. As it is, the creative thinker has to make a decision about his route without having the full information needed for his choice. This dilemma belongs to the essence of creativity.[2]

From the 1950 Webster's New International Dictionary:

> panopticon (pan + Gr. *optikon*, neut. of *optikos* of or for sight). 1. A kind of optical instrument, as a combination of a telescope and microscope. 2. A prison built so radially that the guard at a central position can see all the prisoners. 3. A place where everything can be seen; an exhibition room for novelties.

There is an archetypal poem, and its most ancient design is probably the labyrinth. One suddenly cuts in, leaving the green world for the apparent stasis and darkness of the cave. The first words of a poem propose and nose forward toward a confrontation with what the writer is only partially aware of, or may not be prepared to address until it emerges, flushed forth by digressions and meanders. Poetry twists toward the unknown and seeks to realize something beyond the poet's initial awareness. What it seeks to know might be described as the unlimited interiority of its initial impetus. If a "last line," or "conclusion," occurs to me upon starting to write, I have learned to put it in immediately, so it does not hang before me, a lure, forcing the writing to constantly skew itself so that this "last line" continues to make sense as such.

As far as poetry is concerned, "the bitter combat of the two natures" can be understood as the poet's desire to discover something new or unique vs. the spectral desire of tradition to defeat the new and to continue to assert its own primacy. It is a "bitter" combat because the realization which writing a poem may provide is inevitably partial. The Minotaur is at best crippled, never slain, and the poet never strides forth from the labyrinth, heroic and intact. At best he crawls forth, "wounded" as in the cry of Vallejo in *Intensity and Height*; more often than not, he never emerges at all. The poet never leaves this combat with a total poem, because such a poem would confirm that the discrepancy between desire and the fulfillment of desire had been eliminated. But since my desire is ultimately to create reality and not merely to observe it, I am bound to be defeated if reality is at stake in my poem's ambition. As I emerge from my poem, regardless of what I have realized while in the poem, I am back in the observable biological continuum, and part of it, part of its absolute mortality. I suspect that I am always aware of *this* closure, and that it underwrites (asunderwrites) what I envision while inside the poem.

Harold Bloom's "Six Revisionary Ratios,"[3] which propose to identify "intra-poetic relationships" among the poets that for Bloom constitute an Anglo-American Romantic tradition, may be most useful to poets themselves as a reading of the stages involved in working through a particular poem. Bloom of course intends his "ratios" to challenge current critical attitudes, and as such, it is a book that could only offend poets who are not named as part of the center stage action of Bloom's "tradition," which becomes increasingly arbitrary as it approaches the present. Its argument in which an earlier poet becomes the focus of a struggle on the part of a later poet, who must wrest mana from the former in order to assert himself, is actually depicted by Blake in his vision of his struggle with Milton in *Milton: A Poem*. My idea here is to regard this "struggle" in the context of Fulcanelli's and Ehrenzweig's images of the labyrinth as a symbol of the creative process, in which much more than literary combat takes place. The nodes, or advance positions, that send out radial possibilities everywhichway, are charged with the poet's personal life as well as the context of his times, to mention two considerable influential powers that lie outside Bloom's sense of influence.

Here are Bloom's Six Ratios, followed by the keyword he focuses them with:

1. Clinamen, or Swerve
2. Tessera, or Completion
3. Kenosis, or Emptying
4. Daemonization, or Counter-Sublime
5. Askesis, or Curtailment
6. Apophrades, or Holding Open to the Dead

Is it possible that these terms double Fulcanelli's three-beat rhythm of the labyrinth, offering a more complex and assymetrical sense of the contractions and expansions involved in solving the burden many but not all poems take on?

The poet Swerves into the poem by redirecting his attention from the utilitarian world to one in which "precise subjectivity"[4] is constantly at stake. Or think of the poet as a falling angel who refuses at the last moment to continue to fall and become one of the fallen (=unimaginative man, the literal minded, one for whom the objective world is the real world). He Swerves, beating his wings up, up, up, and enters a new space.

The Swerve into imaginative space together with the first few words or lines, determine mode, tone, direction, and some of the difficulties to be undertaken. Once all of this is in place the poem runs the risk of lapsing into a conventional handling of its direction, in effect Completing itself before it has even gotten underway (as a joke poorly told may imply it punchline and thus be "over" before its actual punchline falls). While the taking on of direction is necessary, if the direction takes its theme or subject matter for granted, the reader has "heard it before," and the poem no longer belongs to itself. Thus the initial move toward Completion must be redirected, or complexed, in order to build up steam, or availability to the unknown that is beyond the poem's initial knowing. Such a move is a contractive one, and would be the Emptying, or willingness to introduce contradiction and/or obscurity via sound-oriented or associational veers.

Emptying makes it possible for the poem to have space for the other or the otherness that can be the most single compelling moment in composition. Daemonization (in contrast to demonization) is the admitting of unconscious material into the composition-in-process, the point at which the poet weds himself, consciousness and unconsciousness fuse—the poet is the world, no separation between his skin and everything else. The eagle of inspiration has sunk its talons into the poet's shoulders and he is borne aloft. There are many ways to approach this moment: in Blake it would be the moment in which the authors in eternity communicate to mortal secretary William. In D. H. Lawrence, the moment that the wind does blow through him (Lawrence states the archetypal daemon plea in: "Not I, not I, but the wind that blows through me!"[5]). García Lorca, weary of hearing critics and conventional poets prattle about the Muse and the angel, borrowed from the world of Flamenco dancing the figure of the "duende," which translates into English rather poorly as "imp." It is a figure of the blood for Lorca,[6] an uprushing or seizure, in which the dancer and poet is momentarily possessed, or incubated (as if by a dream succubus, who lays a psychic egg in the dreamer's body as she fucks him, and "steals" his semen).

Daemonization is perilous because as such it cannot complete the poem (when we are stoned, daemons seem to rush through us, but when we try to articulate their message-sensations, we have nothing—if not less than nothing, for the Daemon of Marijuana loves to gobble up imaginative potential, eating the poem on the spot that had we not gotten stoned might have been *written* the following day). Curtailment is similar to Emptying, in that both are experienced as severe, contractive moments—however, Curtailment is more complex, because the poem has taken on much more burden and possibly unmanageable material than earlier. If the poet does not successfully separate himself from the Daemon's embrace or claws, one result is that inspiration turns into ego-inflation (nearly always just around the corner in Whitman or Ginsberg). In Curtailment (Bloom's Ratio term, Askesis, is based on "ascetic"), the poet must cut into his own beanstalk, bringing the drama tumbling down or seeing into the meaning of the action in Giant Castle through a narrowing, densifying perception. Or to put it another way: in Curtailment, I step outside the poem and in a sense become my own critic, looking for loose ends, ego-inflations that have gotten into the Daemonization, gaps to be plugged—while at the same time I must stay with the shape of the energy recast by the Daemonization.

Bloom's Apophrades is a marvelous image. The dead, the great dead, return to inhabit our houses—life returns to before that fall in which a Swerve was a possibility. The dead return—the poem is over, *the way things are* overwhelms metaphor. The poet, like a streaker now, shows himself to the dead, a phantomic act the dead could care little about. The dead return, life returns to its deadliness, its obliviousness to poetry. Our poems end because at Curtailment we know we cannot escape the product of the poem if we are to have art at all; we know we cannot sustain the poem against the desire of the dead to reinhabit the *temenos* they believed they inhabited in their own time. In a great closure (Wallace Stevens' "Each person completely touches us/With what he is and as he is/In the stale grandeur of annihilation."[7]) there is a shadowed Daemonization, an embrace at the edge of here and not-here.

The dead are now back in our houses. We are outside, outsiders to the poem, peripheral, schizophrenic, caught up in the physical need to reconnect. Every completed poem collects its rejected children, bundles them into its immense laundry-basket and takes off. Image of its huge ass, in peasant shoes, hurrying away from van Gogh's corn field.

Notes

1. Fulcanelli: Master Alchemist, *Le Mystère des Cathédrales*, London, 1974, p. 48. On the following page, Fulcanelli offers an alchemical definition of Ariadne. "Placements II," in my *The Name Encanyoned River: Selected Poems 1960–1985*, explores the resonance of Ariadne as the "mistress of the labyrinth."

2. Anton Ehrenzweig, *The Hidden Order of Art*, Berkeley, 1971, pp. 35–37. Ehrenzweig's drawing of "the maze (serial structure) on p. 36, reminds me of shattered glass more than of the concentrically infolding/ outfolding labyrinth. See also van Gogh's *Starry Night*, with its two milky flows of light, one curling down to tuck into the other curling up—a figure Wilhelm Reich identified as "Cosmic Superimposition." The so-called "serial poem" (Whitman's "Song of Myself," Jack Spicer's "Books") attempts to make use of nodal discontinuities, viewing sections as corresponding rather than connecting.

3. Harold Bloom, *The Anxiety of Influence*, NYC, 1973, pp. 14–15. The novice must decide to what extent Bloom's highly exclusionary study (in which only several 20th century American poets appear in a context that presents them as representing the end of an essentially English literary tradition) is a projection of his own anxious desire to be with poets, one of them, a poet himself. Is it possible that in failing to realize himself as a poet, he envisions the end of a great tradition in his own time, and appoints himself as the eagle-surveyor on a crag overlooking a battlefield of his own construction that stretches narrowly back to Milton?

4. Robert Kelly's phrase, which will appear in his own context later in *Novices*.

5. *The Complete Poems of D. H. Lawrence*, Vol. 1, NYC, 1964, p. 250.

6. "Theory and Function of the Duende," *Lorca*, The Penguin Poets, London, 1960. See Robert Duncan's novice encounter with Lorca elaborated in the 1972 Preface to *Caesar's Gate*. For distinctions between "daemon" and "demon," see James Hillman's *The Dream and the Underworld*, NYC, 1979, especially the "Barriers" section, which considers Materialism, Oppositionalism, and Christianity. Emily Dickinson's #754, written around 1863, is as severe a description as I know of Daemonization and the extent to which its possession can become a life possession, a living out of an alien other's commands. Lawrence emphasizes unconscious message over the poet's willing; in Dickinson's visionary description, the poet is seen as a tool (a gun), at the trigger-mercy of an owner-duende who can fire her at whim (see Susan Howe's thoughtful and differing consideration of this poem in *My Emily Dickinson*, Berkeley, 1985):

> My Life had stood—a Loaded Gun—
> In Corners—till a Day
> The Owner passed—identified—
> And carried Me away—

And now We roam in Sovereign Woods—
And now We hunt the Doe—
And every time I speak for Him—
The Mountains straight reply—

And do I smile, such cordial light
Upon the Valley glow—
It is as a Vesuvian face
Had let its pleasure through—

And when at Night—Our good Day done—
I guard My Master's Head—
'Tis better than the Eider-Duck's
Deep Pillow—to have shared—

To foe of His—I'm deadly foe—
None stir the second time—
On whom I lay a Yellow Eye—
Or an emphatic Thumb—

Though I than He—may longer live
He longer must—than I—
For I have but the power to kill,
Without—the power to die—

7. Wallace Stevens, *The Collected Poems*, NYC, 1957, p. 505.

Chapter 8

My sense of poetic labyrinth here is very flexible—for one writer "the bitter combat" at the center may fill the stage, and for another opening and/or closure may be so difficult that the other stages seem to be nonexistent. And too, there are experiences of the labyrinth which are not engaged by the use I have made of Bloom's "Ratios." To some extent, the elaboration of any vision is labyrinthine. Olson's vision of Homer's *Odyssey* as a dance-drama, in which a shaman-hero dances his way through a gauntlet of monsters to be reunited with a human other,[1] suggests how labyrinthine a 20 year voyage can be. While a single poem may be experienced as working through a maze, such a poem may also be a mere knot in a network that comprises all the writer's poems as well as his unwritten life. In relation to the labyrinth, I would like to consider one of several existent poetic Curriculums for novices. Unlike the others I will mention later, it is not a set of proposals or even an argument, but a tilting assembly of names, subjects, and ideas that evokes the accesses and restrictions of the labyrinth itself.

Charles Olson's "A Plan for a Curriculum of the Soul" may be especially baffling for the novice accustomed to poetry anthologies that for the most part contain poems which the editors feel are self-contained, and can be examined and taught as discrete objects. Poets who tend to write discrete lyrics (Robert Herrick, Emily Dickinson, Robert Frost) can be fairly represented in such anthologies. Poets whose work is primarily constellational—in which individual poems refer not only to themselves but are part of the diagram of a larger constellation—are poorly represented. This is a primary reason, in my opinion, for bypassing anthologies and reading all poets in terms of individual books that in most cases they themselves organized.[2] This does not mean that such poets as William Blake, Ezra Pound, and Charles Olson only write poems that are referential to their own systems—all three, in fact, have written superb self-contained lyric poems. What it does mean is that to appreciate a passage in *The Four Zoas*, or *The Cantos*, or *The Maximus Poems*, you need to know the way in which the entire poem relates to what has come before and after it in the poet's body of work. Poets who attempt to increase the responsibilities of poetry by drawing upon the materials of non-literary disciplines—who in effect strive for a vision big enough to combat the resistance of their times to poetry—are almost inevitably pedagogical.

On February 9, 1968, Olson sent his student George Butterick a 2 page "outline," that on the one hand was probably spontaneous (reflecting current preoccupations) and on the other the result of 20 years of research and writing. Such a "Plan" suggests a mysterious correspondence between terrestrial labyrinths, star maps, and the human mind. Not only does this "Plan" fail to follow the steps of most outlines, it treats its "subjects" as if they were pick-up-sticks that had suddenly been loosed from the poet's grip, falling everywhichway on the page. The only "direction" is that indicated by the fact that the title, one third of the way down on the right-hand page, is under a phrase ending in the word "completion," suggesting that the "Plan" is to be read as a kind of asymmetrical swirl, working down from the title on the right-hand page, crossing over to the left-hand page and following it upward, then crossing back to the right-hand page and ending with "completion." The problem with following such a direction is that the left-hand page has obviously been written from the top down. Another reading possibility is to disperse with direction entirely, and take the subjects and suggestions as "free bodies" brought together in a single double-page arena. If they are taken as a set of leads, the novice can follow them out himself. By coming to terms with "Alchemy—rather by plates [as connected to dreams]" or with what Olson might mean by "Bach's *belief*," he can (often by arguing with Olson) start to develop his own assembly of intersecting subjects or directions.

how to live as a
  single natural being
    the dogmatic nature of   how many?   *as* _____
      (order of)   & how each
    experience   made known,
               exercised,
                      organs &
Ismaeli muslimism   &, all together,   function - <u>activity</u>
                <u>create</u>   of the <u>soul</u>
Alchemy - rather by plates   <u>organism</u>   or psyche or
                       <u>Heaven</u> or <u>God</u>

    [as connected to dreams]

    pictorialism

       as in Earth, "View"

      & <u>perspective</u>
      /cf. Weyl on ocular
      power

Vision   ✗

    Messages

technically, <u>Analytic Psychology</u>, as only technical study I
know of modern Western man & under enough mental
control   jazz <u>playing</u>

                    dance as individual
                        body-power

equally say Homer's *art*

    Bach's <u>belief</u>

        /cf. Novalis'   <u>Egyptian hieroglyphs</u> (gesture, speech
          "subjects"   -drawing   habits
                            mental condition

    the Norse
        & the Arabs

      -locally, American
        Indians

<u>matter</u>

<u>Phenomenological</u>

<u>Sensation</u>   and   <u>Attention</u>
　　　　　　　　　[training in exhaustion &
　　　　　　　　　　　completion

<u>A Plan for a Curriculum of the Soul</u>

　　　　　　　　　　│　(Intuition　│
　　　　　　　　　　│　& Feeling　│　one's own
　　　the Mushroom │　<u>dream woman</u> │　<u>mind</u> ∧ <u>language</u>

<u>earth</u>　　as a
geology ∧ comprehension like archeology
geography - equally, though here maps & experience of
human history　　　　　　　walking

　　　　　　　ʃin this connection, as habitat
　　　inhabitation of, rather than as politics say
　　　　or national. Instead, <u>physical</u>, &
　　　　<u>vertically incremental</u>

　　　　　　　　　　　　　　　physical
　　man as animal [praxis of - as Earth as a

emotional mental experience

Poets　　as such, that is disciplined lives not
　history or for any "art" reasons <u>example</u>,

Blake ⟩
　　⎿ the same, say, medicine men

　　& like theologians: example, Dante - Giotto

Charles Olson

Butterick objected to the word "drugs" in the copy sent to him
by Olson, and apparently made other objections to the "Plan."
In a letter of February 26, Olson replied:

> Just for further accuracy please change words drugs in 1st line
> of Plan for a Curriculum of the Soul to the Mushroom. I find
> your objection, that there is nothing new in the above, a cu-
> rious demand, and not actually relevant, I don't think, to the
> proposal. That is, the need, in fact—or at least what seemed
> to me the gain of this particular spreading was to have a con-
> gestin [sic] which ought to be including and likewise exclusive.
> Or at least that, so placed, it can then be tested for thorough-
> ness. In fact what new is as interesting now as condensation?[3]

It is fascinating to follow out what has been done to date
with Olson's "Plan." It was first published in *Magazine of Further Studies #5*, 1968, and was subsequently taken up as an in-
vestigative poetic "working" by another Olson student (and
the editor of *Further Studies*), Jack Clarke who selected 28 key-
words from the total 223, and after consulting two other students, Albert Glover and Fred Wah, assigned these words to
28 members of the Olson community, with the proposal that
each would write a 20 to 50 page "fascicle" off of that word.
All but 5 fascicles have been written and published (for the
most part in the early 1970s). When all 28 are completed,
along with Olson's *Pleistocene Man* (letters to Clarke, during
October 1965), to be included in the set without a number,
the "Curriculum" will be bound and published as a single volume, each fascicle becoming a chapter.

It is difficult to say to what extent the individual fascicles
are successful; most are novice work, writing by Olson-allied
students who by the early 1970s had only a fragmentary sense
of Olson's body of work and who had not, at least at that time,
found their own footing.[4] Only a handful represent significant
research contributions to Olson's subjects or could be considered engaging collections of poetry. However, more important
than achievement in this instance, is the extent to which the
fascicles demonstrate that there was a circle of novices around
a single poet who cared enough for his vision to contribute up
to 50 pages on a single word of it. Olson did not *assign* the
fascicles; they were generated by the students themselves. In
response to my letter inquiring as to what use had been made
of the "Plan" and the fascicles, Clarke replied:

Actually, there has been no thought of "use" of it, only a place to be together, the O-community i.e., those living in his "world," his "soul." After his death in 1970, we all needed something to survive the boredom of what was to follow i.e., *before the war*, as Duncan says. We will soon publish the definitive text of *Dante* [Duncan's fascicle, #8], replacing both the earlier fascicle and [the poem in] *Groundwork*, to be sold modestly as "book," i.e., that will be Glover Publishing *for* the Institute of Further Studies.

Notes

1. For Olson's perceptive notes on the Upper Paleolithic, see *Olson* #10, 1978, Storrs, CT. Ten issues of *Olson* were researched, edited, and annotated by George Butterick as part of his own poetic apprenticeship. Butterick, who also edited and annotated over 4000 pages of Olson's poetry, prose, and correspondence, died of cancer in July, 1988, at 46. While he wrote poetry at many points over the two decades of his full-time Olson scholarship, he gave Olson all the front burners, modestly placing his own poems on back ones. Butterick's gesture is tragically moving and perhaps unique in a world in which most novices, sidestepping the risks of a prolonged apprenticeship, only find time for themselves.

2. Other reasons to avoid anthologies: teachability is a prime consideration (how much Stein, Zukofsky and Spicer do you find in current anthologies?)—especially as the selections move toward the present, easy-to-read poems that follow in the wake of the established teachable masters are the rule. The editors are not entirely to blame (though nearly all of them go along with the situation), as trade publishers rely considerably on reports from the field (who the professors want to teach) when they decide whether or not a particular anthology (after production and often high permission fees) will make a profit. While minority poets appear with increasing regularity, many appear to be selected on two bases: they will give the anthology a democratic appearance, and they will not offend Professor X because the poems selected read like the poems of their mainstream male writing-workshop contemporaries.

3. When looking at someone's outline or program for others, it is important to decide if their own poetry and poetics back it up. Olson's concern with "spreading," "congestin," and "condensation" have underpinnings in his work at large. The "Plan" is one of many manifestations of Olson's attempt to revision life as turning on a single center, with the poet as integral to a will to cohere. The "Plan" thus embodies the tension between his extensive "spread" of historical and interdisciplinary materials, and his ongoing "condensation" of his findings. See "The Gate and the Center" essay in *Human Universe*, NYC, 1967. Unfortunately, like most poets of his generation (Robert Duncan being

a striking exception), he assumed a male reader. Thus in the "Plan,"
men are identified as individuals e.g., Bach, Blake, Dante, Novalis,
Weyl—and women generically as Woman.

4. The Institute of Further Studies fascicles are as follows:

#1 *The Mushroom*, by Albert Glover, 1972.
#2 *Dream*, by Duncan McNaughton, 1973.
#3 *Woman*, by John Wieners, 1972.
#4 *Mind* (assigned to Robert Creeley).
#5 *Language* (assigned to Edward Dorn).
#6 *Earth*, by Fred Wah, 1974.
#7 *Blake*, by John Clarke, 1973.
#8 *Dante*, by Robert Duncan, 1974.
#9 *Homer's Art* (reassigned to Alice Notley).
#10 *Bach's Belief* (assigned to Robin Blaser).
#11 *Novalis' "Subjects,"* by Robert Dalke, 1973.
#12 *The Norse*, by George Butterick, 1973.
#13 *The Arabs*, by Edward Kissam, 1972.
#14 *American Indians*, by Edgar Billowitz, 1972.
#15 *Jazz Playing*, by Harvey Brown, 1977.
#16 *Dance*, by Lewis MacAdams, 1972.
#17 *Egyptian Hieroglyphs*, by Edward Sanders, 1973.
#18 *Ismaeli Muslimism*, by Michael Bylebyl, 1972.
#19 *Alchemy*, by David Tirrell, 1972.
#20 *Perspective*, by Daniel Zimmerman, 1974.
#21 *Vision*, by Drummond Hadley, 1972.
#22 *Messages*, by James Koller, 1972.
#23 *Analytic Psychology*, by Gerrit Lansing, 1983.
#24 *Organism*, by Michael McClure, 1974.
#25 *Matter*, by John Thorpe, 1975.
#26 *Phenomenological* (assigned to Joanne Kyger).
#27 *Sensation*, by Anselm Hollo, 1972.
#28 *Attention*, by Robert Grenier, 1985.

Chapter 9

Gary Snyder:

What You Should Know to Be a Poet

all you can about animals as persons.
the names of trees and flowers and weeds.
names of stars, and the movements of the planets
               and the moon.

your own six senses, with a watchful and elegant mind.

at least one kind of traditional magic:
divination, astrology, the *book of changes*, the tarot;

dreams.
the illusory demons and illusory shining gods;

kiss the ass of the devil and eat shit;
fuck his horny barbed cock,
fuck the hag,
and all the celestial angels
            and maidens perfum'd and golden—

& then love the human: wives   husbands   and friends.

childrens' games, comic books, bubble-gum,
the weirdness of television and advertising.

work, long dry hours of dull work swallowed up and
    accepted
and livd with and finally lovd.   exhaustion,
              hunger, rest.

the wild freedom of the dance, *extasy*
silent solitary illumination, *enstasy*

real danger.   gambles.   and the edge of death. [1]

The lack of capitals and the presence of periods give this page of Snyder's a modest notational quality, a man sharing his thoughts with you, without broadcasting their importance. At the same time, *What You Should Know* is a tool-kit, a Poetic Curriculum, a several-year study program in nucleus that if followed, in disciplined "ordered derangement" on one's own, might represent a meaningful compromise between the over-socialized university writing programs and Artaud's stark command of no enlightenment other than oneself on oneself, no initiation *period*. Artaud made this statement after having put himself through his own equivalent of Snyder's Curriculum, and after he had been incarcerated in asylums for nearly 9 years, where he had been "initiated" by therapy and electro-shock.

I would like to draw three nodes from Snyder's piece—experience, research, self-regulation—and suggest that becoming a poet is involved with working out a balance, or rhythm, between these three multi-radial activities—

EXPERIENCE: having the courage of your own impulses, getting in "water over your head;" acting out curiosities and responsibilities whenever possible—confronting a friend, telling off an unfair superior, having the abortion etc., rather than non-action that subsequently possesses or leaks into poems

(In Kyoto, 1963, Snyder seemed to me to live like a monk during the week and like a libertine on the weekend—he rose at 4 AM and had a day's study and writing done by late morning; as I recall, afternoons were given to chores, shopping, teaching English as a foreign language. Early rising probably Zen practice, which permeated but did not curtail—)

Snyder at a ranger station in Mt Baker National Forest, 21 years old:

> Discipline of self-restraint is an easy one; being clear-cut, negative, and usually based on some accepted cultural values. Discipline of following desires, *always* doing what you want to do, is hardest.[2] It presupposes self-knowledge of motives, a careful balance of free action and sense of where the cultural taboos lay—knowing whether a particular "desire" is instinctive, cultural, a product of thought, contemplation, or the unconscious. Blake: if the doorways of perception were cleansed, everything would appear to man as it is, infinite. For man has closed himself up, 'til all he sees is through narrow chinks of his caverns. Ah.

> the frustrated bumblebee turns over
> clambers the flower's center upside down
> furious hidden buzzing
> near the cold sweet stem.

In a culture where the aesthetic experience is denied and atro-
phied, genuine religious ecstasy rare, intellectual pleasure
scorned—it is only natural that sex should become the only
personal epiphany of most people & the culture's interest in
romantic love take on staggering size.[3]

RESEARCH: is of course a kind of experience too, but here I
stress finding contemplative territories that have not been
mined (or strip-mined) by other poets, and making them
your own, bringing them into contemporary writing, by poetry or by prose, in order to increase its range of
responsibilities.

This should involve travel, when such territory is visita-
ble. Olson could have gone to the library and read up on
Maya research (in fact, he did, but was so dissatisfied by
what was available that he became all the more obsessed
with going to Yucatan on his own)—however, nearly pen-
niless, he went to Merida and picked up shards rather than
merely examining photos of them.[4]

Penelope Shuttle and Peter Redgrove write that they
went to their College Librarian seeking information on
menstruation because of Shuttle's cramps and depression.
They found nothing that they could use, and thus began
their own research on an area of every woman's experience
that has become an endless lode of discovery for both of
them.[5]

There is something embedded in the nature of poetry itself that yearns to travel and to translate, not merely a foreign text, but the experience of otherness. "The most sublime act," Blake wrote, "is to set another before you." Thus
Bashō's physical urge to get roving one spring morning in
1689 led to his famous *Oku-no-Hosomichi*,[6] the last of several
haibun-haiku hiking journals, a model of layered cultural
awareness, acute observation, and a heart open to tran-
siency and "the modest proportions of human destiny."
"What Bashō doesn't say," writes translator Cid Corman,

"moves at least as much as what he does. One knows his silences go deeper than reasons. And when his eyes plumb words for heart—when the heart holds the island of Sado, locus of exile, at the crest of a brimming sea, and the eye lifts from that pointed violence and loneliness on the horizon to the stars flowing effortlessly up and over and back into the man making vision, who has not at once felt all language vanish into a wholeness and scope of sense that lifts one as if one weighed nothing?" (Here it is appropriate to note especially in the context of *Novices* the distance Corman has traveled from being an apprentice pounded by Olson's injunctions to the author of the just-quoted sentence.)

In 1965 I hitched, bused, and flew to Lima, Peru, to study the worksheets for the poetry of César Vallejo that I had been attempting to translate from error-riddled editions. While the Vallejo part of the trip was utterly frustrating (his widow denying me and all others access to materials that would have enabled translators and scholars to make his achievement available on an international scale), the spirit of Vallejo led me into days of wandering in the worst of Lima's barriadas, and my need to pay my way into experiencing USIS censorship of a bilingual literary magazine I was hired to edit. The context in which poetic research takes place can become as valuable in regard to learning as the project itself.

To only have yourself as subject, novice, is undermining, and it will tend to push you toward an "academic" (= conventional, diminutional) imitation of other poetries. If your attentions are not partially given over to the non- or foreign-literary, the temptation is to read, with blinders, the work of friends and teachers, and to operate under a single canopy of current literary taste.

At 24, Snyder saw experience and research ultimately as irreconcilable opposites: "Comes a time when the poet must choose: either to step deep in the stream of his people, history, tradition, folding and folding himself in the wealth of persons and pasts; philosophy, humanity, to become richly foundationed and great and sane and ordered. Or, to step

beyond the bound onto the way out, into horrors and angels, possible madness or silly Faustian doom, possible utter
transcendence, possible enlightened return, possible ig-
nominious wormish perishing."[7]

In *What You Should Know*, written when he was in his
mid-thirties, Snyder implies that such opposites are contraries (a Blakean perception: two-way traffic without
collisions).

It is risky to go to college and remain there moreorless for
the rest of one's life and expect to write significant poetry.
For the poet, the library is a more intimidating place than a
foreign city, and to spend one's life nursing in a library is not
only to remain an "eternal adolescent" as far as the alleys of
Calcutta are concerned, but to become so overwhelmed by
what one does not know—can never know—that what one
intuits, or does at least deeply feel, gets trashed. Great writing involves protecting one's intuitions, even one's ignorance. Knowing, as such, is not always an advantage to making significant art. Acknowledging one's ignorance, and
learning to respect personal as well as human limitations,
while one works with the welter of fantasies that tumble between certainty and helplessness, is not learnable in school,
and can probably best be dealt with in what I would call
"neutral solitude" (Rilke's little château in the Swiss mountains, Blake's flat in "fourfold" London, Artaud's cell at
Rodez). For a poet, ignorance is as deep a well as knowing,
and lifelong adherence to institutions of higher learning
(with travel contingent upon awards) not only wrecks any
possible balance between the two, but puts the poet, daily,
class-wise, office-wise, library-wise, before the dragons of re-
spectability and caution.[8]

The poetry and prose of William Bronk is a testimonial
of the extent to which ignorance can be fugally held in an
imaginative frame.

Again, Artaud (he is contemplating van Gogh): "No one
has ever written, painted, sculpted, modeled, built, or in-
vented except literally to get out of hell.

And I prefer, to get out of hell, the landscapes of this
quiet convulsionary to the teeming compositions of

Brueghel the Elder or Hieronymous Bosch, who are, in comparison with him, only artists, whereas van Gogh is only a poor dunce determined not to deceive himself."[9]

SELF-REGULATION: I take the term for this third "node" from the psychology of Wilhelm Reich, who believed that "the function of the orgasm" was to enable an individual to respect and take responsibility for his own energy household. Reich envisioned a world that did not need regulation from without (the police, the state, the nation), but a world in which people enjoyed their work because they had chosen it as an outgrowth of what Snyder refers to as "the discipline of following desires" (in contrast to negative self-restraint). In contemplating an ideal world made up of self-regulatory people, Reich was elaborating one of the core perceptions in Blake's poetry:

> What is it men in women do require?
> The lineaments of Gratified Desire.
> What is it women do in men require?
> The lineaments of Gratified Desire[10]
>
> (1793)

—a way of erotically grounding the Golden Rule, as it were; physical gratification as a *requirement* (note how trenchantly this word clings in the line, in contrast to "want" or "need") of the human, identical for both sexes, a reciprocity. Neither Blake nor Reich saw Gratified Desire or self-regulation as an end in itself—both saw it as a requirement for giving oneself wholeheartedly to one's work, whether that work be farming or sculpture. In my own life (partially through 2 years of Reichian therapy, 1967–1969), I have discovered that there is an "antiphonal swing" (I coin the phrase off the last line in Hart Crane's *The Bridge*) between gratificational love-making and imaginative release, that these two "acts" are contraries, not opposites, and that as in the alchemical image of the "double pelican," they both feed each other in contrast to sapping strength from each other.

That which helps us define what we are also marks out boundaries. What we are not, artistically-speaking, is a limitation. The challenge is to create a self that is up to, and imaginatively includes, all the selfhood and selves one has experienced. Even if we are able to allow contradiction and flow of contraries in our work, each assertion, each place-ment, carries, like an aura, its unstated qualification or ex-ception. In my own case, this challenge is: how accommo-dating can I be to material that flies in the face of my "antiphonal swing?"

Crane's "Havana Rose" recalls a conversation with the bacteriologist Hans Zinsser over dinner at a restaurant in Havana, 1931:

> And during the wait over dinner at La Diana,
> the Doctor had said—who was American also—
> "You cannot heed the negative—, so might go on
> to undeserved doom . . . must therefore loose yourself
> within a pattern's mastery that you can conceive, that
> you can yield to—by which also you
> win and gain that mastery and happiness which
> is your own from birth."[11]

For 30 years, I have thanked Crane for having the savvy to write down Zinsser's words (whose "undeserved doom" Crane met within a year of that dinner), which offer yet an-other image of the labyrinth, as a pattern one masters and works (dances) within (Olson's: "how to dance/sitting down"). My own attempt at a "pattern's mastery" is sounded by the three words I have been mulling over in this section, words that make up a kind of web, or trampoline, I have constructed between sky and earth, and one which, against which, by which, I have lived and worked since the late 1960s. To these three words, I would now add a fourth: EX-PERIMENT, the poetic engagement with the sustaining mesh of experience-research-self-regulation. One's eyes bouncing off one's sheet of typing paper, one's mind against the trampoline, hurling one's self-in-process at it again and again, aware that often one smacks and loses balance, falls through a hole and probably wrongly scrambles to get back to what one knows—

> work swallowed and accepted
> and livd with and finally lovd.   exhaustion,
> hunger, rest.

Notes

1. Gary Snyder, *Regarding Wave*, NYC, 1970, p. 40.

2. The discipline of self-restraint vs. the discipline of following desires is taken up by the German painter Max Beckmann in one of a series of open letters that he wrote "to a woman painter" in 1948 while he was in residence at Stephens College, in Columbia, Missouri. Beckmann writes:

> It is necessary for you, you who now draw near to the motley and tempting realm of art, it is very necessary that you also comprehend how close to danger you are. If you devote yourself to the ascetic life, if you renounce all wordly pleasures, all human things, you may, I suppose, attain a certain concentration: but for the same reason you may also dry up. Now, on the other hand, if you plunge headlong into the arms of passion, you may just as easily burn yourself up! Art, love, and passion are very closely related because everything revolves more or less around knowledge and the enjoyment of beauty in one form or another. And intoxication is beautiful, is it not, my friend?
>
> Have you not sometimes been with me in the deep hollow of the champagne glass where red lobsters crawl around and black waiters serve red rumbas which make the blood course through your veins as if to a wild dance? Where white dresses and black silk stockings nestle themselves close to the forms of young gods amidst orchid blossoms and the clatter of tambourines? Have you never thought that in the hellish heat of intoxication amongst princes, harlots, and gangsters, *there* is the glamour of life? Or have not the wide seas on hot nights let you dream that we were glowing sparks on flying fish far above the sea and the stars? Splendid was your mask of black fire in which your long hair was burning—and you believed, at last, at last, that you held the young god in your arms who would deliver you from poverty and ardent desire?
>
> Then came the other thing—the cold fire, the glory.
>
> Never again, you said, never again shall my will be slave to another. Now I want to be alone, alone with myself and my will to power and to glory.
>
> You have built yourself a house of ice crystals and you have wanted to forge three corners or four corners into a circle. But you cannot get rid of that little "point" that gnaws in your brain, that little "point" which means "the other one." Under the cold ice the passion still gnaws, that longing to be loved by another, even if it should be on a different plane than the hell of animal desire. The cold ice burns exactly like the hot fire. And uneasy you walk alone through your palace of ice. Because you still do not want to give up the world of delusion, that little "point" still burns within you—the other one! And for that reason you are an

artist, my poor child! And on you go, walking in dreams like my-self. But through all this we must also persevere my friend. You dream of my own self in you, you mirror my soul.

Perhaps we shall awake one day, alone or together. This we are forbidden to know. A cool wind beyond the other world will awake us in the dreamless universe, and then we shall see our-selves freed from the danger of the dark world, the glowing fields of sorrow at midnight. Then we are awake in the realm of at-mospheres, and self-will and passion, art and delusion are sinking down like a curtain of grey fog . . . and light is shining behind an unknown gigantic gleam.

There, yes there, we shall perceive all, my friend, alone or to-gether . . . who can know?

[Tr. by Mathilde Q. Beckmann and Perry T. Rathbone]

Art, then, for Beckmann, seems to spring from between self-re-straint and following desires in at times a nearly helpless way to make contact with "the other," not as a love slave, but on a spiritual plane. Snyder's *discipline* of following desires proposes a "way"—Snyder is a Buddhist—that would be flexible enough to include art and a living other.

3. Snyder, *Earth House Hold*, NYC, 1969, p. 19.

4. For Olson in Yucatan, see *Letters for Origin*, and Vols. 5 and 6 of *Charles Olson & Robert Creeley: The Complete Correspondence*, Santa Barbara, 1983 and 1985, as well as the essay "Human Universe," in *Human Universe*, NYC, 1967.

5. Penelope Shuttle & Peter Redgrove, *The Wise Wound: Menstruation and Everywoman*, London, 1986.

6. *Back Roads to Far Towns*, Bashō's *Oku-no-Hosomichi*, NYC, 1968. A landmark in the translation of Japanese haibun and haiku. For impro-visations on haibun in English, see the 6 Haibun in John Ashbery's *A Wave*, NYC, 1984. Direct imitations of haiku in English are generally of little interest; however, many of Corman's very short poems are keen workings off haiku sensibility and form, e.g.,

> The cicada
> singing isnt:
> that sound's its life

(from *for granted*, New Rochelle, NY, 1967). Haiku suggests that all event is spontaneous and that dramatic narrative is an accordion-ex-pansion of a shakahachi flute-shriek moment.

7. Snyder, *Earth House Hold*, p. 39.

8. In his *The Life of John Berryman* (London, 1982), John Haffenden wrote: "He belongs to what has become known as the Middle Gen-eration of American poets, a group that includes Delmore Schwartz, Robert Lowell, Randall Jarrell, and Theodore Roethke." While

"confessional" (a term I believe coined by the poet and critic M. L. Rosenthal) is a fuzzy identifying term for these poets, much of their writing is characterized by personal trauma felt as *the* centripetal force that whirls all other considerations of myth, learning, and daily observation, into its vortex. Refusing la vie bohème, expatriotship, and engagement by non-English European literary movements—Berryman it seems might have improved his lot by becoming a Dadaist—these poets stayed home, looked up to Yeats, Auden and Frost, and established the image of the American poet as a teacher sharing an office with his academic colleagues, a very tactile member of a middle-class professional community. Because of the congruity of these poets to the teaching profession itself, and because their writing for the most part does not provide any challenging difficulties, it is natural that they have been taught a great deal, identified by teacher-critics as *the* poets of their generation, and are presented in the majority of textbook poetry anthologies as the creators of post WW II American poetry.

9. *Antonin Artaud Selected Writings*, NYC, 1976, p. 497.

10. *The Complete Writings of William Blake*, London, 1957, p. 328. For Reich on self-regulation, see *The Function of the Orgasm*, NYC, 1961, pp. 143–161.

11. *The Poems of Hart Crane*, NYC, 1986, pp. 200–201.

Chapter 10

Snyder's *What You Should Know* is the child of post-WW II interdisciplinary, experimental, experience-oriented poetics, a new American poetry, open to (and often weakened by) cross-cultural appropriations. In his broad and thoughtful essay, "The Poet & the City," (1962), W. H. Auden proposed a more traditionally Western Curriculum, what he called his "daydream College for Bards:"

1. In addition to English, at least one ancient language, probably Greek or Hebrew, and two modern languages would be required.
2. Thousands of lines of poetry in these languages would be learned by heart.
3. The library would contain no books of literary criticism, and the only critical exercise required of students would be the writing of parodies.
4. Courses in prosody, rhetoric, and comparative philology would be required of all students, and every student would have to select three courses out of courses in mathematics, natural history, geology, meteorology, archaeology, mythology, liturgics, cooking.
5. Every student would be required to look after a domestic animal and cultivate a garden plot.[1]

Auden's "College," with its emphasis on memorization which has become archaic in our time, is a model for poet as Man of Letters, a Jack of All Literary Trades, who elaborates his life in poetry, letters, reviews, essays, possibly editing and translating etc. Relative to Snyder's *What You Should Know*, it is Ivory Towerish; at the same time, it implicitly believes in a continuity of Western literature and humanities that have become suspect to Snyder with his Eastern focus aligned with Zen Buddhism and underscored by a belief in a usable shamanic deep past. Snyder's program is thus more tied to present-day consumer society and to the deep past than is Auden's, which spreads out in the immense Western "interval" between. Snyder's poet is a ronin (a masterless samurai) with his house on his head; Auden's a broadcaster at the console of the great Western Library, with a house or cottage to stroll home to in the evening. Broken down into the most rudimentary forms, Snyder is a hunter, Auden a planter.

While pondering poetic Curriculums, I recalled Robert Graves' *The White Goddess*, a scholarly Fantasia on the nature of "true poetry," in which Grave's picture of ancient Celt and Irish poets carries not only Auden's erudition but also Snyder's shadow of "the dancing sorcerer," the Upper Paleolithic shaman of 15,000 BC (a figure involved with the whole rope of a clan's knowledge and ability to survive, in contrast to the contemporary American poet who at best represents one strand of a rope unraveled throughout the humanities, medicine, magic, and law):

> The ancient Celts carefully distinguished the poet, who was originally a priest and judge as well and whose person was sacrosanct, from the mere gleeman. He was in Irish called *fili*, a seer; in Welsh *derwydd*, or oak-seer, which is the probable derivation of "Druid." Even kings came under his moral tutelage. When two armies engaged in battle, the poets of both sides would withdraw together on a hill and there judiciously discuss the fighting. . . . The gleeman, on the other hand, was a *joculator*, or entertainer, not a priest: a mere client of the military oligarchs and without the poet's arduous professional training.
>
> In ancient Ireland the *ollave*, or master-poet, sat next to the king at table and was privileged, as none else but the queen was, to wear six different colors in his clothes. The "bard," which in medieval Wales stood for a master-poet, had a different sense in Ireland, where it meant an inferior poet who had not passed through the "seven degrees of wisdom" which made him an ollave after a very difficult twelve-year course.
>
> Who can make any claim to be a chief poet and wear the embroidered mantle of office which the ancient Irish called the *tugen*? Who can even claim to be an ollave? The ollave in ancient Ireland had to be master of one hundred and fifty Oghams, or verbal ciphers, which allowed him to converse with his fellow-poets over the heads of unlearned bystanders; to be able to repeat at a moment's notice any one of three hundred and fifty long traditional histories and romances, together with the incidental poems they contained, with appropriate harp accompaniment. . . . to be learned in philosophy; to be a doctor of civil law; to understand the history of modern, middle and ancient Irish with the derivations and changes of meaning of every word; to be skilled in music, augury, divination, medicine, mathematics, geography, universal history, astronomy,

rhetoric, and foreign languages; and to be able to extemporize poetry in fifty or more complicated meters. That anyone at all should have been able to qualify as an ollave is surprising; yet families of ollaves tended to intermarry; and among the Maoris of New Zealand where a curiously similar system prevailed, the capacity of the ollave to memorize, comprehend, elucidate and extemporize staggered Governor Grey and other early British observers.[2]

Graves will go ahead through his charming, questionable, vexing, and thoroughly labyrinthine work to argue that all "true poetry" celebrates some incident or scene of a particular story, identified in the chapter entitled "The Single Poetic Theme:"

Originally, the poet was the leader of a totem-society of religious dancers. His verses—*versus* is a Latin word corresponding to the Greek strophe and means "a turning"—were danced around an altar or in a sacred enclosure and each verse started a new turn or movement in the dance. The word "ballad" has the same origin: it is a dance poem, from the Latin *ballare*, to dance. All the totem-societies in ancient Europe were under the dominion of the Great Goddess, the Lady of the Wild Things; dances were seasonal and fitted into an annual pattern from which gradually emerges the single grand theme of poetry: the life, death and resurrection of the Spirit of the Year, the Goddess's son and lover.

Poetry began in the matriarchal age, and derives its magic from the moon, not from the sun. No poet can hope to understand the nature of poetry unless he has had a vision of the Naked King crucified to the lopped oak, and watched the dancers, red-eyed from the acrid smoke of the sacrificial fires, stamping out the measures of the dance, their bodies bent uncouthly forward, with a monotonous chant of: "Kill! kill! kill!" and "Blood! blood! blood!"

Constant illiterate use of the phrase 'to woo the Muse' has obscured its poetic sense: the poet's inner communion with the White Goddess, regarded as the source of truth. Truth has been represented by poets as a naked woman: a woman divested of all garments or ornaments that will commit her to any particular position in time and space. The Syrian Moon-goddess was also represented so, with a snake head-dress to remind the devotee that she was Death in disguise, and a lion crouched faithfully at her feet. The poet is in love with the White Goddess, with Truth: his heart breaks with longing and love for her. She is the Flower-goddess Olwen or Blodeuwedd; but she is also Blodeuwedd the Owl, lamp-eyed, hooting dismally, with her

foul nest in the hollow of a dead tree, or Circe the pitiless fal-
con, or Lamia with her flickering tongue, or the snarling-
chopped Sow-goddess, or the mare-headed Rhiannon who
feeds on raw flesh. *Odi atque amo:* "to be in love with" is also
to hate. Determined to escape from the dilemma, the Apol-
lonian teaches himself to despise woman, and teaches woman
to despise herself.[3]

If poetry did begin in a matriarchal age, and if the first poets
were women, how could their source be the Muse Graves iden-
tifies as *the* Muse for the heterosexual male poet? Graves would
of course argue that regardless of cultural gender-priority the
first poets were male—in fact, he goes a good deal further, by
stating that "woman is not a poet: she is either Muse or she is
nothing."[4] But since men are the guardians of attitudes and
laws in a patriarchal culture, it is reasonable to assume that
women would be the guardians, and shamans, of what appears
to be ancient Indo-European matriarchal culture.

I suspect that the matter is much more complex than this,
and offer the following suggestion: in an Upper Paleolithic
semi-nomadic hunting-based clan, the magic of the kill would
be primarily man-determined and the domain of a male shaman. On the other hand, the magic of generation (fecundity,
birth, the hearth) would be primarily woman-determined and
the domain of a female shaman. The gender emphasis of Upper
Paleolithic image-making is clearly matriarchal, and is associated with cave shelter (the so-called Venuses were found in
rock shelters, either as a carved part of the shelter, or stuck
into the shelter floor) or deep-cave sanctuary; it stresses fecundity and the "Demeter delta," or yonic triangle. There are,
however, male images too: more often than not animal-
garbed, dancing figures whose animal attributes or associations
appear to be tied up with the hunt and power over hard-to-kill
beasts.[5]

Graves' book is, in fact, an amazing mish-mash of personal
projections and ollave-like research, and I would not reject all
of his detailed evidence for a view of poetry based on a White
Goddess, who at one time may have been as cogent a source
for imagination as Jesus Christ was for Renaissance painters.
But always White? Whiteness is but a portion of the spectrum
attributed to The Triple Goddess (the precursor figure for the

Christian Trinity), "a Goddess in three aspects—as a young woman, a birth-giving matron, and an old woman. This typical Virgin-Mother-Crone combination was Parvati-Durga-Uma (Kali) in India, Ana-Babd-Macha (the Morrigan) in Ireland, or in Greece Hebe-Hera-Hecate, the three Moerae, the three Gorgons, the three Graece, the three Horae, etc. Among the Vikings, the three-fold Goddess appeared as the Norns; among the Romans, as the Fates or Fortunae; among the druids, as Diana Triformis. The Triple Goddess had more than three: she had hundreds of forms."[6] In the margin of the "Fates" entry page of Barbara G. Walker's *The Woman's Encyclopedia of Myths and Secrets*, I scribbled various attributes of the three phases of The Triple Goddess:

1. lily dove white purity spinner frog spider silver fish white stag silver wheel white-flower virgin creator
2. rose passion red measurer heifer serpent dragon preserver
3. darkness black cutter sow vulture sphinx black bitch mare destroyer [Homer's black ewe which Odysseus sacrifices in order to speak with Tiresias in the 11th book of the *Odyssey*]

Relative to the amazing rainbow of The Triple Goddess, to simply call her White is to remove her from the dimensionality of red and black (the Venus of Laussel, carved in the prow of a tiny rock shelter in the French Dordogne at around 20,000 BC was originally painted red). And might there not be Brown Goddesses? Yellow Goddesses? Blue Goddesses? "The White Etc Goddess," Olson is said to have commented.

And the homosexual poet? In Graves' categorical patriarchal (matriarchally veiled) thinking, he is Apollo-bound, and without a "true" source, or figure, of inspiration. Yet for both García Lorca and Robert Duncan, to mention two homosexual *and* Dionysian poets, the source is neither Muse nor angel, but the figure so compellingly described by Lorca as the "duende," the daemonized thought of the blood.

And lest Apollo be implicitly dismissed by Graves' dismissal of him from the "truth" of poetry, the novice should consider Walker's entry on "Abaddon" in her *Encyclopedia*, which describes the first spirit-pits, which seem to float in time between the Upper Paleolithic cave-sanctuaries and the pagan temples, of which medieval cathedrals and modern churches appear to be the final "installments:"

The god Apollo was a solar king in heaven during the day, and a Lord of Death in the underworld at night. His latter form became the Jewish Apollyon, Spirit of the Pit (Revelation 9:11). Apollo-Python was the serpent deity in the Pit of the Delphic oracle, who inspired the seeress with mystic vapors from his nether world. The Greek word for Pit was *abaton*, which the Jews corrupted into Abaddon—later a familiar Christian synonym for hell.

Also called a *mundus* or earth-womb, the *abaton* was a real pit, standard equipment in a pagan temple. Those who entered it to "incubate," or to sleep overnight in magical imitation of the incubatory sleep in the womb, were thought to be visited by an "incubus" or spirit who brought prophetic dreams. Novice priests went down into the pit for longer periods of incubation, pantomiming death, burial, and rebirth from the womb of Mother Earth. Once initiated in this way, they were thought to gain the skill of oneiromancy: the ability to interpret dreams.

The Old Testament Joseph earned his oneiromantic talent by incubation in a Pit. The "brothers" who put him there seem to have been fellow priests. He could interpret Pharaoh's dreams only after he had submitted to the ritual. Assyrian priests derived similar powers from a sojourn in the Pit. They then assumed the priestly coat of many colors, signifying communion with the Goddess under her oneiromantic name of Nanshe, "Interpreter of Dreams." It seems likely that Joseph's coat of many colors would have been given him originally not before the initiation but afterward, by a "father" who was actually the high priest.[7]

The Irish ollave in his six-colored garb, priest Joseph in his many-colored coat, against the backdrop of a primordial spore in which clear skies and the moon, night and the bottomlessness of source, fire and the blood of renewal as well as the blood of destruction, are "the deeds done and suffered by light."[8]

Notes

1. Auden's essay is from *The Dyer's Hand and Other Essays* (NYC, 1962); it is reprinted in *Poetry and Politics*, NYC, 1985, pp. 36–51.

2. Robert Graves, *The White Goddess*, NYC, 1969, pp. 21, 22, and 457.

3. Graves, *The White Goddess*, pp. 422 and 448. Graves' dancers, turning and twisting as we poets intend our lines to imaginatively turn and twist, are also figures of the labyrinth, an out-in-the-open version of its interior action: after the elevation of Dionysus and Ariadne as a

divine couple into the night sky, Theseus and his companions are said to have danced a swirling in and out dance around a horned altar, which recalls the actual bull horns through which Cretan bull-dancers flipped in a sacred marriage of the sun-king and the moon-goddess.

4. Graves, *The White Goddess*, p. 446.

5. S. Giedion's *The Eternal Present*, Vol. 1, *The Beginnings of Art*, NYC, 1957, is an excellent introduction to Upper Paleolithic imagination. See also Olson's lectures in *Olson #*10, and my *Fracture*, Santa Barbara, 1983.

6. *The Woman's Encyclopedia of Myths and Secrets*, NYC, 1983, p. 1018.

7. *The Women's Encyclopedia*, pp. 2–3.

8. Goethe is said to have stated: "Colors are deeds done and suffered by light."

Chapter 11

When I briefly notice a comment or gesture, and then dream a variation of it, I feel there is something nourishing going on. Caught up in the flux of consciousness, the figure has been encouraged to perform a version of itself in a way I failed to imagine until my rational intentionality and its attendant guards fell asleep. Merely noticed, or overheard, the figure was a black spot. The dream tells me that such a spot is a spore with fungus potential, like one of those firecracker worms, a small keg that upon ignition curls out several inches. Such a spot, placed on the warmer of Psyche, is capable of its own elaboration.

Another kind of dreaming seems to be an intensification of ordinary dreaming, capable of a hallucinatory welding of waking imagination and dreaming. If there is a pattern to such dreams, they seem to occur around dawn after I have awakened from an ordinary dream. I find myself wondering if I am awake or still dreaming. I am suddenly as if awake in a dream, or dreaming awake, and I have only to reclose my eyes to see what is behind my consciousness at that instant. Since there seems to be nothing on my mind, the spurt of images feels completely spontaneous (as if I were projecting a movie onto a screen out of my head, a movie of unconscious action that bypassed conscious censorship). I find myself in a corridor or tunnel of parthenogenesis, in which being there is sufficient to produce "the whole show." There is the sensation of head as camera projecting a tunnel of light in which it creates its own action, of rapid passage around bend after bend (it is, I think, on this basis that I referred to images as winding windows earlier). There is a curious wholeness or freedom in poetry that seems contingent upon consciously/unconsciously recreating these conditions while writing.

Such dreaming evokes a line of Pound's in Canto 92 in which he states that while Paradise is not artificial it *is* jagged (and a line or two later, indicates that the jaggedness is the jaggedness of lightning, which recalls a line of Dylan Thomas's: "The meaning of miracle is unending lightning"). Such dreaming is extremely physical—it pours through my body like tons of grain through a sieve in a way that recalls the second hour of LSD sensation. It suggests that the tough material world is actually highly porous, combustible, and that anything can become something else instantaneously. It is redolent of both day and night, and while it occurs the partition between desire and the fulfillment of desire is momentarily down.

My first "visionary" dream took place in Kyoto, 1963, when my first wife and I were living on tatami in two rooms of a 19th-century Japanese house. I was daily in the throes of trying to find out what counted for me *and* to articulate it at the same time. I had no confidence in my imagination, so what took place in those long mornings was mainly the typing out of a line or two, and then, blocked, staring at it on the page. A grinding against no self in the hope that a speakable self could be sparked or driven into existence. I often had nauseating headaches and was so tense that I once passed out while reading Blake's *The Book of Urizen*.

I recall at one point a young Japanese man was in the news for having crossed the Pacific Ocean in a small boat. I was struck by this, without knowing why, and typed out:

Kenichi Horie, across the Pacific, alone

I must have stared at the line for a week, unable to push on. I felt that I knew nothing about the ocean, or sailing, or who Horie was, or what his act *meant*. It did not occur to me that I had some things in common with the line—I had crossed the Pacific to find myself in a foreign world facing a long and perhaps very lonely voyage. Looking at such a line, it was as if heavy tongs gripped my head from behind, paralyzing my mind while they held me in position before it.

In April of that year, I became aware of the following pattern when I stretched out on the futon to sleep: as I was about to doze off, I would hear a sharp PING that rang in or was struck off my forehead between my eyes. At first this "bell" was more frightening than I can describe. In an effort to escape it, I would concentrate on falling asleep. In doing so, a second thing would happen: as if from about 100 feet away, there was the sound of a window being slammed shut, as if someone with both hands had slammed a window as hard as possible. I curled tighter into myself and awaited the nightmare. The third phase was the rerun of a "visionary" dream: I was in a twisting tunnel moving at high speed, head first, with a sense of impending collision, as if the only culmination could be a shattering. The tunnel was smoking, and in attempting to see through the fumes, and in effect get to the tunnel's end before it got to me, I would conjure my father's face. The dream would always end before I reached the end of the tunnel and I seemed to be in the tunnel a bit longer each time the dream occurred. It was as if I was on some sort of psychic hamster-belt being run through my paces night after night until a certain charge exhausted itself.

Was I repeating emerging from my mother to instantly become dependent upon my father to catch my "fall?" My father, who had whipped me, and was never, after infancy, a loving companion? There was a peristaltic ambivalence in the dream, roller-coaster exhilaration and fright. I began to realize that for the psychological background of the dream to be activated, there had to be a present condition to supply its terrible energy. Besides the mental tension of sitting blocked before a page, there was a concomitant physical tension/distraction: I would often become sexually aroused, or feel a need to defecate. Since I did not desire my wife or feel it was right (or have the nerve) to be unfaithful, I tried to swallow the sexual sensation and keep concentrating on the page in the typewriter. At one point, for several months, I spent time at the Kyoto University Library, making use of a huge Spanish dictionary, in order to check hundreds of words in the poetry of Vallejo which I had begun to translate daily in the fall of 1962. In 1965, back in Indiana for the year, I tried to simply say what those days in the library had been:

> The Library
>
> Either masturbate or sleep—
> that's how it was translating Vallejo those days,
> an interlude coming along the railing back
> looking down into the court. A pine
> low-flung & stately. Below it benches
> a student or two. But the book, the

heavy leather Spanish dictionary
I could not crack. Nor "the book is
the life blood of a master spirit." It was
reliving days I never got in then,
days that could not be relived,
days & days, & the past came up,
without my present how alone I was,
how singular & horny. Love was not
given at home. Stiff at night I was
swollen in the morning. I ached.
& Vallejo lay mute. The john
walls stared What do you want
coming here? Why are you not
at home without literature
and life?[1]

The traditional Japanese toilet is what is referred to in the West as a "Turkish toilet"—one squats over a rectangular porcelain trench. When I got up from sitting cross-legged on the tatami by my typewriter table to relieve myself, I would find, once crouched in the benjo, that I did not have to go at all. It occurred to me that there was a bizarre relationship between the position assumed by the Aztec goddess of childbirth and filth, Tlazolteotl-Ixcuina, squatting in the tension of birth, with a little male figure emerging between her knees, and my own position, caught up in attempting to birth myself, which on a psychic level had become a caricature of projecting a poem onto the page. To find the Aztec metaphor obviously did not solve my problems, but it helped me to realize that in making a life-commitment to poetry I had brought to the surface lower-body tensions that I had been unaware of before. It slowly began to dawn on me that everything was at stake in the creative act, that what I did or did not do with myself away from working on a poem was going to attach itself to the writing process, and, furthermore, it was best to try and work through these problems away from the writing table so as to not ultimately have to transcend them in the act of writing (and thus live with them unresolved) if for no other reason than that I could not stand facing them day after day while attempting to write.

About six months before the bell-slammed-window-roller-coaster nightmare, I had a hallucinatory experience that seemed to loosen me up to the extent that such a nightmare could occur. Snyder, who was living half an hour north of us with his wife, the poet Joanne Kyger, had urged me to try LSD, having tried it himself after either Leary or Alpert had passed through Kyoto with the newly-discovered drug. Because of all the difficulties I have briefly described, I was afraid something awful would happen to me after Snyder told me that I would see all my demons if I took LSD. But I said no, even though I was desperate and *feared* that LSD might tear the potential poet in me apart.

A month after having rejected Gary's offer, I spent the better part of a night drinking sake with some strangers in downtown Kyoto bars, and dreamed that night of Snyder in a kind of steamshovel contraption being lowered right over a felt-covered gambling table where he picked up gold coins with his buns (it was Halloween, and the night before, Barbara Eshleman had given her Junior High-school English students an apple-bobbing party). I awoke with a potent hangover, and early in the afternoon motorcycled to a bar dormitory where I was to meet a male friend who managed a hostess bar. The dormitory Mama-san informed me that my friend was not in, but invited me in anyway for cookies and tea. She sat me down before a TV set and left the room. There was a teen-age adventure movie on, in which, during a track meet, a fat boy tried to climb a pole, and failed, to the glee of his peers. While watching this scene, I suddenly thought of Robert Kelly (who weighed 400 pounds in those days), and was moved to tears over what I took to be Kelly's difficulties as a man and as a writer. I left the dormitory after an hour or so, feeling so sensitive it was as if my nerves were in the very surface of my skin.

I decided to cycle out to the Snyders for an impromptu visit, and again found that the person I had come to visit was not home—but Joanne was, and again I was invited in for tea. We sat at the kotatsu for an hour or so, discussing Jung and a few of his hard-to-grasp terms. I left near dusk, and started home. Cycling down Junikendoori, a wide commercial avenue, I suddenly began to hallucinate: the motorcycle became an ox, its handlebars ox horns; a lumber yard turned into a manger in which I saw wise men kneeling by the infant Jesus. At first I tried to hold on and will myself home, but by the time I got to

Nijo Castle, I was afraid I was going to have an accident, so rather automatically I decided to circumambulate the Castle, and left the cycle in the tourist-bus parking-lot. At the point I started around the square moated medieval structure, everything was roaring with transformation, and anything I looked at instantly turned into something else. At one point I saw Kyger's eyeballs in the moat. At the far northwest corner of the Castle, I looked up into the sky and saw a human-sized bright-red spider about 30 feet up in the air, drawing thread out of its spinnerets and weaving itself into pulsating, quilt-like, luminous dusk sky. The appearance of the red spider was the sublime moment of the experience; it signified to me that I was being offered my poetic totem, and thus confirmed that I was a poet.[2]

I did take LSD in the spring of 1965, and in reflecting on the experience[3] it occurred to me that Joanne Kyger could have put LSD in my tea. I asked her about this in 1977; she gave me an equivocal answer.

The red spider confirmation was more than a poem—and less than one too. It gave me crucial support and justified my efforts to keep on trying to write in a "grasping for straws" time, when every day was a maze of conventional dead-ends and self-destructive lures.

Notes

1. *Indiana*, Los Angeles, 1969, p. 28. See also "The Octopus Delivery" in *Coils*.

2. For more on the red spider, see "The House of Okumura VI" in *Coils*, "The Book of Coatlicue" in *El Corno Emplumado* #14, and previously cited "Placements II" in *The Name Encanyoned River*.

3. In a short essay entitled "Novices," written in 1963 and published in *matter* #3, Robert Duncan writes: "Three sources from which our imagination draws: the sensory universe about us, the works of man and the dream. Of a fourth, 'hallucination' or 'vision,' I am shy, and have few coordinates. I once in near trance 'saw' a man of fire; again, in a mescaline experiment conducted by the Stanford University pharmacy school, I saw the tree of life, but it was a 'work of man,' a figure in a vast weaving, weaving itself, and/or a living mosaic . . .
   [But Charles Olson, in Buffalo, would not accept my using 'hallucinate;' and now, searching out the word I find it means (*alucinor*, to wander in mind, to talk idly—might this really be: *to talk oneself into?*—prate, dream; and back of the Latin, Greek: ἀλύσις, distress,

anguish. To be beside oneself with grief, see things in that light) O.E.D.: To be deceived, suffer illusion, entertain false notions, blunder, mistake. Wow! no wonder Charles didn't want it.]"

Yet wandering in mind would seem to be an accurate description of creative fits and starts, "life in the labyrinth," and anyone who has ever had a conversation with Duncan himself has experienced the poet's associational weaving/wandering. Frye, in distinguishing Blake as a visionary (in contrast to a mystic or madman), gave that word status, but one wonders: is the tree full of angels glimpsed by the young Blake of a different order of seeing than Duncan's man of fire? In our Protestant society, visions induced by hallucinogens tend to be suspect, but even a cursory glance at world mythology and shamanic activity will show the novice that in a pagan or primitive context the mushroom is viewed as an aid in seeing, an intensifier of visionary potential. Olson himself experimented with hallucinogens, and "Maximus, from Dogtown—II" appears to be written under their sway.

My first LSD experience in the spring of 1965 was an extraordinary experience (its hallucinogenic core is worked into "Origin," *Coils*, pp. 94–95); subsequent experiences with the drug were less rewarding.

Chapter 12

The poet's resistance to psychoanalysis is a resistance to discovering his unconscious motives for writing poetry—as if discovering a severing—a witch with a long nose intruding into the play-house window, discovering what the children are "really" doing there. The fear that more information is the end of information is Blake's enemy, "doubt which is self-contradiction," and it hamstrings the novice through developing a reluctance to investigate Psyche—to investigate *anything*.

But I want to cut across what I believe here, and let a poet who rejected analysis and who went ahead to write magnificent poetry after doing so, speak:

Rainer Maria Rilke to Lou Andreas-Salomé, 1912:

> I rather shun this getting cleared out and, with my nature, could hardly expect anything good of it. Something like a disinfected soul results from it, a monstrosity, alive, corrected in red like the page of a school notebook.[1]

> I do feel myself infinitely strongly bound to the once begun, to all the joy and all the misery it entails, so that, strictly speaking, I can wish for no sort of change, no interference from without, no relief, except that inherent in enduring and final achievement. . . . It seems to me certain that if one were to drive out my devils, my angels too would get a little (let us say), a very little fright and—you do feel it—that is what I may not risk at any cost.[2]

Rilke would agree with Auden about allowing no books of criticism in a College for Bards, and, like Rimbaud, is concerned with the monstrous, but from a differing angle: Rimbaud intends to *infect* himself to undermine the starched domesticity of Charlesville and make contact with the chthonic powers of poetry. Rilke fears the *disinfected* soul that might result from analysis, as if it could empty him back to the military-school classroom where he was at the mercy of a master's formulaic revisions. By offering his devils (hardly daemons here; more likely neurotic habits) to a Freudian analyst, he fears that he will be removing an essential alchemical component from the compost he needs to nurture his angels, or flowering. For disinfected Rimbaud, ensouling is a reinfecting; on the other hand, Rilke, probably more abused and disoriented by education than Rimbaud, now seeks to protect what he has been able to save of himself. Infection and disinfection coil like snakes about the caduceus of a healing that for the poet is never clearly one or the other.

In 1922, having weathered this critical period of his life without succumbing to analysis, Rilke wrote to another correspondent:

> I believe that as soon as an artist has found the living center of his activity, nothing is so important for him as to remain in it and never go further away from it (for it is also the center of his personality, his world) than up to the inside wall of what he is quietly and steadily giving forth; his place is *never*, not even for an instant, alongside the observer and judge. . . . Most artists today use up their strength in this going back and forth, and not only do they expend themselves in it, they get themselves hopelessly entangled and lose a part of their essential innocence in the sin of having surprised their work from outside, tasted of it, shared in the enjoyment of it! The infinitely grand and moving thing about Cézanne. . . . is that during almost forty years he remained uninterruptedly with his work, in the innermost center of it—, and I hope someday to show how the incredible freshness and purity of his pictures is due to this obstination: their surface is really like the flesh of fruit just broken open—, while most painters already stand facing their own pictures enjoying and relishing them, violating them in the very process of the work as onlookers and recipients. . . . (I hope, as I say, someday convincingly to point out this to me absolutely definitive attitude of Cézanne's; it might act as advice and warning for anyone seriously determined to be an artist.)[3]

Artaud

> I don't want to eat my poem, I want to give my heart to my poem.[4]

For Rilke, the labyrinth of the creative process is a walled monastery, out of which fans the heretical world of analysis, worldly fame, hubris, enjoyment, and relishing. While the present is not walled off from the past, inspiration is to be protected from its correctives, as if it takes its orders from a source that regards forays into its inversions, opposites, and caricatures, as blasphemous (elsewhere Rilke praises Cézanne for not losing an afternoon of painting even to attend his only duaghter's wedding).

Rilke's words are profound and brave, and speak from an ability to sustain himself in a solitude that most American artists would find pathological (so gregarious are we, or, in alchemical terms, such "leaky vessels"). However, I see a long-standing problem in removing the poet from a realm that includes correction, self-observation, and judgment. As a European poet born in the 19th century, who made good use of some of the last aristocratic patronage, Rilke participates in a removed, high Romantic image which regards the poet as spontaneous and visionary, a receptacle through which a primordial frenzy speaks itself. In a "classic" statement of this viewpoint, Jung, in 1922 (the same year Rilke wrote his mature masterpieces), declared: "as long as we are caught up in the process of creation, we neither see nor understand; indeed we ought not to understand, for nothing is more injurious to immediate experience than cognition."[5]

But there is a shadowy side to this viewpoint: if the poet does not "see" or "understand" while writing, such seeing and understanding will have to be done for him. As one with "special access to the beyond, he is from a societal viewpoint put in the same category with the child, the insane, and the primitive and, at one time, women,"[6] and thus ultimately in need of correction or criticism. He is only to be trusted at the point his writing is rationally framed, canonized, and thus sheared of the fangs that made him special in the first place. Living poets, from this viewpoint, are better off dead, when the irrational and disturbing aspects of their writing have been drained off. A second shadow is this: those who do the draining and evaluating cannot be creative, because spontaneity and self-involvement would weaken critical judgment. For several hundred years, poets and critics have been snapping at each other across a narrow but deep river. The living presence of the poet vexes the critic who is unsure of what to do with him as he has no historical perspective on him. The poet, on the other hand, not only finds it disgusting that someone outside his "divine frenzy" should be allowed to judge him (and in effect decide whether he is to be read or not by future generations), but suspects that the critic is a "closet" poet who does not have the guts to lay himself bare.

In 1984, I recorded several hours of conversation with the Archetypal Psychologist, James Hillman, whose thoughtful and creative books I have been reading for the past decade. We wanted to start to build a bridge across the river I have briefly described, feeling that poetry and psychology can make use of both banks. Neither of us believe in what Hillman refers to as "a certain court model, which splits consciousness from un-consciousness, reason from unreason, creation from criticism." His response to the Jung passage quoted here is as follows:

> I wouldn't agree with that. I would say that when you're in the midst of the process of—I don't want to use the word "creation" either, it tends to get inflated—but in the midst of writing, or speaking a poem, or whatever, let's just say writing, there is a seeing going on in the hand and in the heart, and in the eye, which is not the kind of seeing Jung is talking about which is detached outside seeing, but the fingers have an eye in them. E-Y-E. An eye that knows to put this word and not that word and to cross that out suddenly and to jump to the next thing. That's all seeing. It's not blind. That's a romantic sense that there's natural creativity and then there's detached scientific observation.

In regard to his own practice of analysis, Hillman commented:

> I think most of these alternatives come into the analytical room, especially the one of being a scientific detached judge/ critic/observer. Certainly that is a favorite stance one takes in being an analyst. But it is not the only story at all. There's also the talking from that place Rilke is talking about, when you're absolutely inside the image, or inside the emotion or complex that's in the room with the two of you, maybe it's come out of a dream, maybe it has just come out of sitting there and what is said is very free. And now: *is* it blind? . . . are we where Jung said you don't know what you're saying and you don't see what you're doing? I don't think that's the case. I think it's very much like I said. Your fingers have eyes in them. And when you're reacting emotionally and imaginatively to the dream, you are doing the same thing as Rilke is talking about. There is a poe-

sis. You are making a whole new construction, which is not an interpretation. It's a new construction that's closer to what you do when you translate . . . but let's get rid of that word "interpretation," and maybe even "translation." For the moment, that isn't what I want to do with this dream that is coming. I don't want to *interpret* the dream. I want to talk to the dream, talk about the dream, restate the dream, imagine from the dream, but I don't mean a free-floating fantasy. And I sure don't mean a bunch of subjective reactions and feelings and associations: "This makes me think of . . ." You are there, I believe, to *respond* to the dream, and that forces you to stick pretty close to it, much as you have to with a poem that you are translating. The dream is your master, let's say. It provides the limits, the discipline. What you say to it is in service of the dream. Yet, all along the response comes from the imagination.[7]

Robert Kelly:

> *The Subjective*
>
> is not the opposite of the rigorous.
> It is the most rigorous, the most difficult.
>
> The *precise subjective* is what philosophers are too
> lazy & too generalizing to labor, scientists too
> frightened to search out.
>
> The Objective is p.r. for the Generalization.
>
> Objective Order, so-called, is mental artifact,
>   consensus, "collective consciousness,"
>   "lethargy of custom (STC"
>
> The 'objective' is a consolation prize for those
>   who've lost the real.[8]

Notes

1. *Letters of Rainer Maria Rilke,* 1910–1926, NYC, 1969, p. 44.

2. *Letters of Rilke,* p. 51.

3. *Letters of Rilke,* pp. 273–274.

4. *Artaud Anthology,* p. 101.

5. "On the Relation of Analytical Psychology to Poetry," *The Portable Jung,* NYC, 1972, pp. 301–322.

6. "Part One of a Discussion on Psychology and Poetry," *Sulfur* #16, p. 58.

7. "Psychology and Poetry," pp. 58, 72–73. At other points in our discussion, Hillman unpacks such loaded terms as "divine frenzy" and "primordial," terms whose ultimate effects are as negative as they are charismatic.

8. "On Discourse," *Io* #20 (Biopoesis), p. 18.

Chapter 13

Paul Christensen introducing the first installment of the Edward Dahlberg/Charles Olson Correspondence, in *Sulfur* #1:

> In August, 1936, Charles Olson knocked on the door of a boarding house in the town of Rockport, a mile beyond East Gloucester, to inquire if an Edward Dahlberg were home. The message was sent upstairs, but Dahlberg was keeping to his room to avoid hearing his fellow boarders saw away at their instruments in their weekly home concert in the parlor below. He sent back the message that he was busy. Olson misunderstood and proceeded to wait at the front door until after midnight. Dahlberg was again reminded of his caller at the door, and in a fit of pity and embarrassment rushed down to greet the stranger. He was surprised to find a stalk of a man rising six feet seven inches, a twenty-six-year-old man with huge eyes and bushy eyebrows, enormous hands, with shy, intense, determined gestures. Dahlberg let him in and the two fell into a conversation about Shakespeare in which they forgot the time. Some hours later, Dahlberg let him out again and realized privately to himself he had met someone who had a chance at greatness. In the instant, Dahlberg became a father to this hulk of potential, this handsome, scholarly, awkward figure who was the image of his own youth.[1]

The first time I heard the word "apprenticeship:" Kyoto, 1963, a lithographer friend, Will Petersen, introduced me to a 60-year-old bonsai gardener who was described as the "apprentice" to someone. I later asked Will how old the "master" was. In his late 70s, he said. And then explained: this man will be going off on his own soon and have perhaps 10 years to develop what he has learned.

Elderly Stevens:

> The poem is the cry of its occasion,
> Part of the *res* itself and not about it.[2]

Not, in other words, the cry of the poet himself, a perspective Stevens adopted from the very beginning. For many other poets, the first 10 years of writing seem to essentially be one long cry. There is something compelling and honest about being direct in this regard (e.g., *Howl*), or, as in the case of the first poem in Jerome Rothenberg's first book, allowing the cry but also putting it into a context that offers resonance beyond a self-pitying ego:

'A Little Boy Lost'

They took me from the white sun and they
left me in the black sun, left
me to sleep among long rows of overcoats:
I was a city boy lost in the country, a
wound in my hand was all I knew about willows
Can you understand, do you hear the wide
sound of the wind against the cow's
side, and the crickets that run down my
sleeve, crickets full of the night, with
bodies like little black suns? try as I will
there is only this cry in my heart, this cry:
They took me from the white sun, and they
left me in the black sun, and I
have no way of turning now, no door.[3]

Allen Ginsberg came to the door of his NYC 10th Street flat and told me he would talk with me if I would buy him a hamburger. I did, downstairs in the luncheonette, and he talked nonstop for an hour about Shelley and Mayakofsky. Then he told me to go meet Herbert Huncke and tell him Allen had sent me. I knocked, and was met by a gentle face from the pit who invited me in to a living room in which several people were silently camped out on battered furniture. "We're cooking a poem, man," Huncke said, "com'ere." He led me into the kitchen and opened the oven door. There it was, a typed poem on a sheet of paper turning brown around the edges in a 350° oven. Huncke closed the door and shuffled back into the living room, me following. Still no one said anything. After hanging around for a few minutes, I decided I was definitely not hungry, and slipped out.

Louis Zukofsky took me over to his Brooklyn Willow Street front window and asked me what I saw. I said something about the Statue of Liberty being out there. Zukofsky paused for a moment, and then said: "the statue is in the water." A memorable but dumb remark I decided years later.

Cid Corman was preparing to edit the "second series" of *origin* magazine when I knocked on his boarding-house door in San Francisco, 1960. We had already exchanged a few letters, and one, Corman's response to a group of student poems I had submitted to *origin*, had made me break into tears while I was reading it. In bolt-from-the-blue fashion, it said: get serious about poetry or forget it. When I met Cid, he was brooding about Ginsberg, Burroughs, and the Beats, whom he felt were "sick." The new *origin* series, to be anchored by the serialization of Zukofsky's "A," was to provide an "open" alternative. Eight years later, Corman wrote an "open letter" nominating Allen Ginsberg and Muhammad Ali for President and Vice President of the United States which I published in my magazine, *Caterpillar*.

Corman would respond immediately (his letters seemed to come back approximately an hour after you had mailed yours to him) to anything I said, and while his responses were aggressively pedagogical (some of which was undoubtedly an echo of the pounding he had taken from Olson), he was astute and awesomely dedicated, so when I moved to Kyoto about a year after Cid had, I started seeing him on a regular basis. He would leave his room in the afternoon, browse in the Maruzen bookstore or visit art galleries, eat downtown, and with books, letters, notebooks, etc., "retire" to the Muse coffee-shop until about 11 PM. If you wanted to see Cid, you called on him at his "office" there. Over the next two years, I dropped in once or twice a week, and learned the rudiments of translation and magazine editing. We did a little translating together, and Cid went over the first few drafts of my Vallejo translations. I watched him on a weekly basis assemble issues of *origin*, and would often walk all the way home from the Muse (about an hour) just to digest, slowly, in the night air, passing through temple grounds and narrow fenced alleys, what Cid had said.

At first in Kyoto I tried to imitate the kind of poetry Corman was publishing in *origin*, but doing so was like compressing my body into my eyes, and my eyes into a few, almost factual lines. After 5 hours of evading most of what was on my mind, I would end up with something that gave no indication of *my* situation, or the energy I had put into those 5 hours. At a certain point, I began to feel that Corman was watching me every minute when I was writing (and sometimes when I was not writing: before doing something I found myself asking myself, what would Cid think of this?). Indeed, he was an unyielding advocate of what he himself practiced, but I had set him like a Nevermore-Alter-Ego-Raven on my shoulder, and once I realized that, I was able to start exploring the kind of poetry I wanted to write—which went against Cid and *origin*. In fact, it was much closer to the "sick" poetry of Ginsberg, in that it began to unpack my impacted past and confront my unresolved identity via some of the "unmentionable" areas that I touched on before in *Novices*. My apprenticeship, by the beginning of 1964, consisted of:

1. Visits to Corman at the Muse, and a correspondence with a wide range of poets, including Jack Hirschman, Thomas Merton, Jerry Rothenberg, W. S. Merwin, Robert Kelly, Paul Blackburn, and Mary Ellen Solt.

2. Working on my own poems every morning, then after lunch motorcycling downtown to the Yorunomado coffee-shop where I translated Vallejo until suppertime.[4]

3. After supper, I would walk down the hill to a neighborhood coffee-shop and read for several hours.

4. Besides short poems, I was increasingly caught up in an interminable, meandering long poem, "The Tsuruginomiya Regeneration," which was frustrated by my attempts to investigate the Pandorabox of materials that I had opened in the past five years and, at the same time, to prove to myself that I had successfully changed my life.

Of course I did not stick by this schedule every day; at times the impossibility of making things flow as a poet, translator, or reader, became so frustrating, I would wander around Kyoto looking for places to take hold—things, or incidents, in which I could perceive something and get beyond a literal description. When occasionally reading, observing, and thinking did coalesce, I would find myself propelled forward and up against a new wall, that was often menacing and bizarre:

Paused on the Shichijo Bridge,

      the day misty,
lovely, grisly . . . the Kamogawa fades, shallows forever,
winding out through Kyoto's southern shacks . . .

      below, in the littered mud,
a man stabs around in cans and sewage,
in his ragged khaki overcoat and army puttees
I was taken forward to a blind spot

      (he pulled himself up
a rope ladder hung over the stone embankment
and with limp burlap sack slung over his shoulder
disappeared down an alley
home?   to the faces?
              What do
I express when I write?
   Knives?   or Sunlight?
              And "everything
that lives is holy" raced through my mind

      Walking home,
paused under the orange gates of Sanjusangendo, in
under the dripping eaves, cosy,
I noticed a strand of barbwire
looped over stakes I had stepped
inside of

      and then it came to me)
      I would kill for you[5]

At the moment of this realization, "you" was my wife Barbara,
and after writing these lines I mainly felt that I had contained
the sensations of those 30 minutes on the bridge. Years later,
I realized that the stakes I had stepped inside of were the stakes
of a commitment to poetry, which Psyche warned me was as
severe as taking or protecting life.

    *

Snyder once told me that I was spending too much time on
Vallejo and not enough time on Eshleman. I responded that
by working on Vallejo I was working on Eshleman—and I
think I was right, but I also think Gary's challenge is
meaningful.

Unfortunately, each novice has to determine, "without having the full information needed for his choice," how to con-
stellate his own field, knowing that an immense amount will
be left out. In my own case: would I have been better off studying Pound than Vallejo? Or doing zazen at Daitokuji instead of
reading *The Masks of God*, or Frye's *Fearful Symmetry* on which
I spent a full year? How could I have possibly launched into a
long poem (roughly 400 pages), without a thorough study of
epic poetry and subsequently tracking the evolution of the "serial poem," from Whitman, say, to Spicer? Like many other
modern poets, I have made intuitive moves, trying to honor
obsessions, and staying away from areas that did not compel
me. I have taken the risk that by following my own energies I
would in the long run create a more genuine, and hopefully
enduring, constellation of nodal emphases, than I would by
respecting Anglo-American canons and studying them to the
exclusion of peripheral and even inconsequential materials. If
something has felt like an energy deposit, a metaphoric vault
glinting with possible ore, I have swung over to it, forgetting
about what I *should be* doing.

*

At the end of "People," Robert Creeley writes of:

> the
>
>> one
>> multiphasic
>> direction,
>>
>> the going,
>> the coming,
>> the lives.
>>
>> *I*
>> fails in
>> the forms
>>
>> of them, I
>> want
>> to go home.[6]

Under all of our outward reaching, our attempts to contact
what we are not, to elephant-trunk the brush into our maws,

there is this countercurrent, this back-pulling creature, so as-
tonishingly evoked by Ferenczi, seeking home, and what really
is home—for a poet? What really is home for one involved
with a labyrinth that turns in as it turns out, and for whom
center is mainly divergence, that inner/outer arabesque, both
van Gogh and Reich presented as a cosmic and human core?
I want to go home—but is not home for the poet a being in and
with a "multiphasic" configuration, an abode in imagination,
and how different is it from the cradle, how different is the
mental sensation of a poem going at full tilt from the boiled
eggs my mother would bring to me in the middle of the night
when at 10 years old I would awake and cry and cry until she
would cook something and attend me?

"My house is not my house," Lorca wept, so we could say
that our home is not our home, and is the home that is not a
home something like the Zen *Mumonkan*, the gate that is not
a gate, the "gateless gate?" I have this continuing deep intuition that as I curve out, throwing my crab claw imagination
out and out for the prey of material, there is another claw curv-
ing back under me that flows outward as the grasper for material swings back in with its "catch." My feelings about this
are primarily anchored to one experience:

Soon after I started trying to write poetry, in 1957, I met a
slightly-older couple, George and Dolly Stewart, who lived in
Indianapolis, at a party in Bloomington, and made friends
with them. I began to visit them on a regular basis, driving up
from Bloomington, and staying with them over the weekend,
without letting my parents, 20 minutes north of the Stewarts,
know that I was in town. Both George and Dolly were painters,
and in their sensual, bohemian apartment, permeated with the
aroma of pigments, I felt deeply at home—even on their
living-room couch I slept a deep, deep nourishing sleep. I left
Indiana in 1961 for the Far East, lost contact with the Stewarts, and when I returned, in 1964, they were no longer in
Indianapolis.

Near the end of my mother's life in 1969, while visiting her
and my father before they sold the family home and moved
into a nursing-home, I suddenly became curious as to where I
had spent my second and third year. I knew the location of the
place to which I had been brought home from the Methodist

Hospital, and the location of the rental where we had lived during my fourth and fifth years before moving to 4705 Boulevard Place, our one and only house and home. My mother's health and memory were failing, and she agreed: if we were going to find the place, it was now or never.

We drove to a neighborhood south of us that had changed considerably over the past decade, circling around block after block, with my mother commenting how strange everything looked. She said she only recalled that it was a large second floor apartment facing Delaware Street. At a certain point, she said: stop—I think that's it. She was staring at a large nondescript house, which had been broken up into first and second floor apartments. It meant nothing to me, but since we were there, I thought, well, make something out of this, at least go up and walk around it. My mother preferred to sit in the car, so I walked up to the house and moseyed around it. At the southeast corner, there was a public side-door. I opened it and looked up the staircase—and then decided to climb, feeling as I ascended, a strange yet pleasant buoyancy. I thought: my god, she's really found it—and then—I nearly dropped in my tracks, for as my head came up to the level of the landing, I found myself staring at George's and Dolly's door. I looked again: the diagonal crack in the interior panel had been painted over but it was still there.

My distressed mother could have been mistaken in regard to finding the house we lived in when I was two—but she did bring me to the place to which I had been magnetized, my chrysalis, as it were, at the point I broke free of college life in Bloomington and sought a new place in poetry. And if this house was indeed the house we moved to in 1936 (and why not give her the benefit of the doubt—her lifelong strength had resided in mothering intuitions), then she had effected a kind of *hierosgamos*, or "sacred marriage," taking my point of poetic discovery (Bloomington) in one hand, and the place where she had taught me the rudiments of speech in the other, introducing me to their fusion in that home within home I had unconsciously chosen in which to incubate myself at the point that I desired that nebulous regeneration that still drips like blood through the sidewalks of clouds.

O ripe husk within ripe husk,
    way by which we would bury ourselves in
        the active tomb of
            our earliest attempt
                at speech.

Notes

1. The complete correspondence between Olson and Dahlberg (published in *Sulfurs* #1–3) is a moving example of the near-impossibility of apprentice and master recasting their roles in an eye-to-eye relationship at the point the apprentice becomes the equal of his teacher. In the eyes of the master, the apprentice never quite comes up to him, reciprocity from his viewpoint representing a serious diminution of his size. In the eyes of the apprentice-become-equal, the master's values have been surveyed and found wanting (their gaps are space, in effect, for his growth), thus his earlier size was a mirage. Entangled in this whole matter of course are the spectres of natural father and son (or mother and daughter). Olson in 1953, speaking to students at Black Mountain College as he reflects on Cro-Magnon man:

> What I want to pose to you now is: what is your experience of your size? do you, or not, move among the herd of men with the sense of yourself as not yet filling out your size? do you, thus, have the feeling of being smaller, both than yrself and than how others appear to you? The problem is best measured in terms of that illusion of the parents. And that question, are we ever fathers or mothers to ourselves? Actually, I take it, we aren't—that our omnipotence is only always in the eyes of the children of us, not in ourselves except as—because we once were—our parents had that dimension. I have this hunch: that the reason why grandfathers and grandmothers were up until recently lent an authority was that, in fact, only in that third generation do we acquire some of that dimension the first generation seems to have in the eyes of the second—and of course, there is cause of a subtler order than the biological: that by grand time any of us ought, if we have managed our lives, to have filled out more of those outlines of our possibility we are strained toward. But the living question stays, am I right that most of our time we take ourselves to be smaller than others, to be smallness in face of the world?
>
> (Olson #10, pp. 31–32).

Vallejo in 1937 Paris:

> The accent dangles from my shoe;
> I hear it perfectly
> succumb, shine, fold in the shape of amber

and hang, colorific, evil shade.
My size thus exceeds me,
judges observe me from a tree,
they observe me with their backs walk forward,
enter my hammer,
stop to look at a girl
and, before a urinal, raise my shoulders.

For sure no one's at my side,
I could care less, I need no one;
for sure they've told me to be off:
I feel it clearly.

The cruelest size is that of praying!
Humiliation, splendor, deep forest!
Size now exceeds me, elastic fog,
rapidity hastily and from and joined.
Imperturbable! Imperburbable! They ring
at once, later, fatidic phones.
It's the accent; it's him.

(Conductors of the Pit, p. 24)

2. Wallace Stevens, *The Collected Poems*, NYC, 1957, p. 473.

3. Jerome Rothenberg, *White Sun Black Sun*, NYC, 1960.

4. The psychological crux of translation as it pertains to apprenticeship is addressed by Eliot Weinberger: "The dissolution of the translator's ego is essential if the foreign poet is to enter the language—a bad translation is the insistent voice of the translator." (*Works on Paper*, NYC, 1986, p. 132) I have not expounded on my apprentice relationship to Vallejo's European poetry here, as it is amply discussed elsewhere, mainly in the Introduction to *The Posthumous Poetry*, and in three of my own poems: "The Book of Yorunomado," "At the Tomb of Vallejo," and "The Name Encanyoned River."

5. From "The Book of Yorunomado," *The Name Encanyoned River*, p. 23.

6. *The Collected Poems of Robert Creeley*, Berkeley, 1982, pp. 494–495.

Appendix

In September 1957, the seventy-four-year old William Carlos Williams was interviewed by John Wingate (standing in for Mike Wallace) on the national CBS television program "Nitebeat." As Williams' biographer Paul Mariani writes, "Wingate's questions were provocative, teasing, even entrapping, as the portion of the transcript that appeared in the New York *Post* for Friday, October 18—and which Williams used in *Paterson 5*—will show at a glance. Even the caption, 'Mike Wallace Asks William Carlos Williams Is Poetry A Dead Duck,' suggests the kind of high comedy and cavalier dismissal with which the American poet is normally greeted in his own country."

Paterson 5 appeared in 1958, and sometime between then and the fall of 1959, Cid Corman wrote a "double-take" of the interview, which I published in the first issue of the first magazine I edited, *Folio*, Winter 1960, at Indiana University. The piece has never been reprinted, and I offer it here as a response-to-the-philistines that is still trenchant. It accurately reflects Corman's view that poetry is to be *heard* (sounded) and that its reception and practice engage all of one's life (in contrast to its use in our society for the most part as an occasion to advance personal prestige).

Double-Take: Another Response
(vide, *Paterson V*, Mike Wallace interview)

Q. Mr Corman, can you tell me, simply, what poetry is?
A. No, simply.
Q. Can you tell me, then, ah, complexly or in any way?
A. It is an expression of life.
Q. That's rather vague, isn't it?
A. No, it simply doesnt evade vagueness.
Q. Cant you give me a practical definition?
A. If poetry could be defined, it couldnt exist.
Q. But how do you *know* a poem when you see one?

A. I dont. I listen.

Q. And when you listen?

A. I hear life expressed and in that expression realized; and I am moved and renewed by the experience.

Q. All right. Look at this part of a poem by e.e. cummings, another great American poet:

      etc etc etc

Is *this* poetry?

A. Aren't you begging the question by loading it?

Q. What do you mean?

A. Instead of flattering me by necessarily specious arguments of "greatness," which are certainly irrelevant, or not flattering either to Mr Cummings or myself by your implied sarcasm, your question might in fairness have simply gone:

      Here is some writing by E.E. Cummings, who is a poet
      of some repute. Do you think it is poetry?

Q. Excuse me, then. Would you care to answer the question in your improved version?

A. No. I cant respond to part of a poem as if it were an entire poem. That would be like handing me your brains, if it were possible, or some other less noble part, and saying, Now what do you think of me, in view of my brains, or whatever, as a man? I frankly wouldnt think anything of you. How could I?

Q. But can you *understand* this piece of writing?

A. Yes. Insofar as a fragment can be understood in isolation. I see that Cummings has playfully broken his words upon a typewriter in describing or trying to get at the way a child may sense or treat a cat. At least, he implies the childlike in spelling out the word "c-a-t" and gives a kind of gentle humor in his reorganization of simple words.

Q. Can such devices be considered poetic?

A. Why not? If they are expressive of life; that is, if they realize life in particular moment.

Q. Dont you think they are rather too clever and too eccentric?

A. Perhaps they draw too much attention to the printed page and the effect gained may be relatively trivial. But even in so small a fragment there is gaiety and joy, which cant be denied. And Cummings deserves no less than our support and sympathetic attention for trying to extend the possibilities of expression, since that is tantamount to giving more possibility to our lives.

Q. But do you think people can understand such writing?

A. They can, if they care to.

Q. But shouldnt a word mean something at once when you see it?

A. It should mean whatever it is, when you *hear* it. There are difficulties in poetry, as there are in life. And you will have as much "success" in understanding one as the other to the extent that you confront those difficulties patiently and with all the powers of life at your command.

Q. Isn't that asking rather a lot in reading a poem?

A. I'm not asking anything. You are. If you care to read (to hear) poetry at all, you must give yourself to it—completely, just as it is given to you. If you go to poetry, you have a responsibility to it equal to its own.

*

What follows are two brief reading lists, and a final salute to all of us from Paul Blackburn (1926–1971). The first list is made up of works that I studied as a novice that taught me something about life and poetry, and that haunt me still. The second list is an up-to-date assembly of books that bear upon poetry as I understand it, an assembly that is intended to create a kind of resource indication upon which future poetry might draw.

Bashō's *Back Roads to Far Towns* (Tr. by Corman and Kamaike); Allen Ginsberg's *Howl* (also the Original Draft Facsimile of *Howl*, the annotations to which include Jack Kerouac's "Belief and Technique of Modern Prose"); Franz Kafka's "The Bucket Rider"; Djuna Barnes' *Nightwood*; Vincent van Gogh's letters; William Blake's 1802 letter to Thomas Butts, "Enion's lament" from *The Four Zoas*, and *The Arlington Court Regeneration* painting; Samuel Taylor Coleridge's "Ne Plus Ultra"; Paul Blackburn's "Crank It Up for All of Us, But Let Me Heaven Go"; Basil Bunting's "Chomei at Toyama"; Hugh MacDiarmid's "On a Raised Beach"; *Black Elk Speaks*; Aimé Césaire's "Lynch" (Tr. by Emile Snyder, in *Hip Pocket Poets #2*); Diane Wakoski's "Slicing Oranges for Jeremiah"; Robert Kelly's "The Exchanges"; Jerome Rothenberg's "The Seven Hells of Jikoku Zoshi"; William Carlos Williams' "The pure products of America go crazy"; Louis Zukofsky's A, sections 9 and 11; Henry Miller's "Reunion in Brooklyn"; Wilhelm Reich's *The Function of the Orgasm* and *The Mass Psychology of Fas-*

cism; Vladimir Mayakofsky's "And Yet" (Tr. by Jack Hirsch-
man & Victor Erlich, the version in *Hip Pocket Poets #*1);
Gary Snyder's "The Market"; Pablo Neruda's "Walking
Around" and "Caballero Solo"; García Lorca's essay on "the
Duende," and his "Oda a Walt Whitman"; Hart Crane's
"Lachrymae Christi" and "Havana Rose"; César Vallejo's
"Hay días, me viene, una gana . . ."; René Char's *Hypnos
Waking*; Max Beckmann's *The Departure*; Hieronymus
Bosch's *The Garden of Earthly Delights*; Chaim Soutine's
paintings of hanging fowl; Bud Powell's "Un Poco Loco";
Lennie Tristano's version of "I surrender dear"; Charlie Par-
ker's "Koko"; Shakespeare's *Hamlet*; the following letters by
Rainer Maria Rilke, in vol. II of the Norton *Selected Letters*:
#194, 209, 211 and 218—also his "An Experience" and
"Archaic Torso of Apollo"; Dylan Thomas's "Fern Hill";
Walt Whitman's 1855 original version of *Leaves of Grass*;
Justino Fernandez's *Coatlicue*; Colin Wilson's *The Outsider*;
Northrop Frye's *Fearful Symmetry*; Joseph Campbell's tetral-
ogy, *The Masks of God*; the *I Ching* (Wilhelm/Baynes trans-
lation); *The Bhagavadgita* (Tr. by S. Radhakrishnan); Jean
Genet's *Miracle of the Rose*.

*

S. Giedion's *The Eternal Present: The Beginnings of Art*.
Georges Bataille's *Lascaux* (in concert with Annette Laming's
    Lascaux, and Leroi-Gourhan's *Treasures of Prehistoric Art*).
R. B. Onians' *The Origins of European Thought*.
Weston LaBarre's *The Ghost Dance*.
Mikhail Bakhtin's *Rabelais and His World*.
Barbara Walker's *The Woman's Encyclopedia of Myths and
    Secrets*.
Sandor Ferenczi's *Thalassa*.
N. O. Brown's *Love's Body*.
Charles Olson's *Call Me Ishmael* and *The Maximus Poems*.
*Conductors of the Pit: Major Works by Rimbaud, Vallejo, Césaire,
    Artaud and Holan*.
James Hillman's *Re-Visioning Psychology*.
Louis Zukofsky's *A Test of Poetry*.

Robert Duncan's *Fictive Certainties* (plus "Rites of Participa-
tion" and "The Homosexual in Society").
Andrea Dworkin's *Pornography*.
Shuttle & Redgrove's *The Wise Wound*.
Rothenberg & Quasha's *America A Prophecy*.
Laura Riding's *The Telling*.
Sjöö and Mor's *The Great Cosmic Mother*.
Wolfgang Giegerich's *The Psychoanalysis of the Atomic Bomb*
(unpublished as of this date in English).
Carlos Castaneda's *The Teachings of Don Juan*.
Hans Peter Duerr's *Dreamtime*.
Robicsek & Hales' *The Maya Book of the Dead*.
Gary Snyder's *Earth House Hold*.
Susan Howe's *My Emily Dickinson*.
Eliot Weinberger's *Works on Paper*.
Charles Bernstein's *Content's Dream*.
John Clarke's *From Feathers to Iron*.
Donald Ault's *Narrative Unbound*.

*

The Art

to write poems, say,
is not a personal achievement
that bewilderment

On the way to work
two white butterflies
& clover along the walks

to ask   .
to want that much of it   .

Design by Phillip Bevis
Typography by Wilsted & Taylor
Printing by Malloy Lithographing, Inc.